GRAND DESIGNS AT 25

Quarto

First published in 2024
by White Lion Publishing,
an imprint of The Quarto Group.
One Triptych Place,
London, SE1 9SH,
United Kingdom
T (0)20 7700 9000
www.Quarto.com

A catalogue record for this book is
available from the British Library.

ISBN 978-1-83600-133-1
Ebook ISBN 978-1-83600-134-8

10 9 8 7 6 5 4 3 2 1

Design by Intercity

Group Publishing Director:
Denise Bates
White Lion Publisher:
Jessica Axe
Senior Editor:
Laura Bulbeck
Art Director:
Paileen Currie
Production Controller:
Rohana Yusof

Printed in Bosnia and Herzegovina

WHITE
LION
PUBLISHING

Kevin
McCloud

GRAND DESIGNS AT 25

Game-changing
designs from the
iconic series

Contents

Forewords

The amazing success of *Grand Designs* over the last 25 years is testament to both the original idea and the brilliance of the many gifted people who've worked on the series over the years. Nearly 200 episodes later, and shown around the world, no-one when filming started in the last century could have imagined *Grand Designs* would still be going strong in 2024. The fundamental idea of following a house being built from start to finish, by self-builders throwing everything they have creatively, financially and emotionally at their projects, has connected with viewers for a generation.

There's the architecture, of course, the astonishing design, the innovative building methods and techniques, the cutting edge sustainability that shows the way for the rest of us. Revealed at the end are eye catching, beautifully crafted and absolutely unique places to live. There's no doubting the influence the series has had, with 'a Grand Design' now part of the common vernacular, shorthand for outstanding architectural ambition.

The self-builders are determined to do things differently, to live in a way that hasn't been dictated to them, that fits who they are. Those who have appeared on the series over the years, not just the builders but myriad architects, designers, craftspeople and contractors, these are the heartbeat of *Grand Designs*. It's their commitment, openness and collaboration that gives an emotional anchor to each story and each finished home.

We never know quite what's going to happen over the two, three and often more years of filming each project. The contributors generously allow Kevin and the film crew into their lives, watching as thousands of decisions are made, both right and wrong, and big life events intervene. The two elements, cutting edge architecture and dramatic human stories, combine to make the series what it is. Building your own house is an enchanting idea most of us won't be able to achieve, but we can at least watch others try, and aspire to one day take the leap.

The series has gradually evolved visually, technically, graphically and musically, with steadfast support from Channel 4. Hundreds of staff and crew – from directors to editors, sound mixers to camera operators, runners to commissioners – all have shared their passion and creativity to make *GD* a success. Not least the man who's been there since day one, the brilliant Kevin.

Throughout my dozen years as first Series and now Executive Producer, the series has been a joy to work on, an observational programme without gimmicks and artificial format points. A house is going to be built; we're just along for the ride, there to enjoy the highs and lows, to celebrate the achievement. Long may it continue.

Choosing the outstanding homes for inclusion in this book was a supremely difficult task. With so many terrific projects to choose from over 25 years, it's been a real head scratcher for Kevin and the team. Despite their diversity, we hope you'll agree the final selection captures the true essence of what makes a *Grand Designs* house. If not, well, no problem – after all the series is about individual expression, strong opinions and difficult choices. Enjoy!

John Lonsdale

In 1998 I didn't know anyone who had built their own house. But that summer I visited a friend in Devon whose oak beam house had been designed from scratch by the architect Roderick James. It was light and spacious, with a double-height room that looked over a river. The oak beams made the house feel like part of the landscape, and the layout was perfectly designed for the way we live now. Everybody I know lives in their kitchen, and in this house it was not a boxy extension but the heart of the house.

I was smitten, and on the basis that you should only make TV programmes that you would really want to watch, I came up with the idea that I called *Grand Designs*. We would follow people who wanted to build their own home, from the muddy field to the sparkling finished building. Channel 4 was interested and we filmed a short pilot with a lighting designer called Kevin McCloud who I knew a bit, and had always thought would make great TV. We filmed him walking around a muddy field, talking to a nervous looking couple who were about to sink all their money, and even more of the bank's, into a self-build house in Sussex. Kevin was enthusiastic, gently sceptical and sympathetic to the unique blend of courage and insanity that leads otherwise normal people to embark on building their own house, and he has remained so ever since.

Getting the first series to the screen was a *Grand Design*-like project in itself – none of the houses we followed were on schedule, and we very quickly went over budget. But, like the homebuilders, I had a blind faith that all the pain would be worth it. It was a belief that was challenged when we got to the very end of the much extended schedule, and the majority of the houses were not ready for the all-important 'reveal'. This was a disaster; I knew that the magic of *Grand Designs* lay in the happy ending when after all the miserable weeks in a freezing caravan, living off instant noodles, the front door would open and our subjects would walk into their 'finished' dream house. Luckily I had been to enough magazine shoots to know that with a few props and some cunning camera angles the camera can lie very effectively. Kevin, with his theatre background, had no problem in visualising the finished houses, and at long last the show was in the can.

Most TV is ephemeral, but what is so wonderful about *Grand Designs* is that it speaks to a basic human fantasy that never fades. The eclectic variety of houses on offer – the house in the woods, the straw house with rats in the walls, the Huf house – has made us all think a bit harder about the kind of place we want to live in. In 1998 I didn't think that I was making an educational programme, but 25 years later I am proud to have been the midwife of a show that has had a real effect on the way we think about architecture.

Daisy Goodwin

Organised chronologically from the first year of *Grand Designs*, in 1999, these outstanding houses represent my selection of game-changers over the decades.

1999
—
Water Tower Conversion
—
Amersham

•	Episode aired	1999
•	Location	Buckinghamshire
•	Owner(s)	Andrew and Deborah
•	Architect(s)	Andrew Tate of TateHindle Ltd
•	Build cost	£500,000 (as of 2024)

Twenty-five years ago, Deborah and Andrew purchased a tapering, 30-m (100-ft) tall brick water tower complete with vertiginous gantries and ladders. At the time, the couple were in their thirties with three children under the age of three. It was not an obvious lifestyle choice, but they were both admirably able to see past the perils of toddlerhood and think long term.

They set about building a capacious, light-filled open-plan extension from concrete-filled polystyrene formwork, glass walling and a concrete slab roof. 'We wanted to live in a space where we could see the children at all times while letting them have some freedom,' Deborah explains. The structure went up in just four months, with Deborah project managing the build and Andrew, an architect, applying his knowledge of commercial building techniques to the site.

As the children grew up, the intention was to convert the adjoining water tower into bedrooms and to divide the living space with internal walls. However, as time passed, they found the uninterrupted views through the building and out into the landscape beyond were too good to obscure. 'The light in this space is really quite magical,' says Deborah.

Instead, the whole family adapted to life in one large space, with the three children sleeping in the study, and Andrew and Deborah sleeping in the living room. 'We had a really big bedsit for five years,' says Deborah who attributes the children's close relationship and 'highly developed negotiating skills' to their communal living arrangements. 'They're also very loud,' Andrew adds. 'They've grown up having to project their voices across the space, so they don't really understand what a whisper is!'

As more funds became available, Andrew and Deborah were able to convert the first two floors of the tower into three separate bedrooms: a temporary room for them (which, post-bedsit, Deborah describes as 'blissful'), a shared room for the boys and a room for their daughter, Freya. 'On our first night in the tower, we heard this thump, thump, thump,' Deborah recalls. 'It was Freya dragging her mattress downstairs so she could sleep with the boys.'

The final phase of this iterative project – 'the icing on the cake' – was the creation of the couple's own two-storey suite at the top of the tower. From here, they are rewarded with views that cover 1,000 square miles.

'Most of the houses are below the tree line,' explains Andrew. 'Looking out, it's as though there's nothing but trees between us and the towers of London.' Another less expected reward is the inherent level of fitness they have both acquired from climbing the 80 steps to bed. 'We take it for granted,' says Deborah, 'but if we're walking upstairs with other people, we really notice the difference.'

Besides the gradual adaptation of the tower, little else has changed internally. They have upgraded the condensing boiler and manifold system that powers the underfloor heating, but the formwork, the green roof and the protective green bank of earth that wraps around the sunken front elevation of the building, all keep them warm in winter and cool in summer. The tower also has a funnel effect, meaning they virtually never need to heat the bedrooms.

Beyond the glass walls their garden remains 'field-like' – a planning stipulation at the time of purchase. Hedges have softened the appearance of their extension and two courtyard gardens have been lovingly cultivated. 'I think if we were going to move, the most important thing would be the connection between the inside and the outside space,' says Deborah. 'In fact, if we decide to do it all again, we have talked about finding the perfect garden because – in the time we have left – we could build a beautiful property, but we couldn't grow a beautiful garden.'

Now grandparents, the home they created for their own children is being put to good use by the next generation of toddlers, who are free to scoot safely around the open-plan space. Seeing how their unconventional space has adapted to the changing family dynamic has provided both Andrew and Deborah with decades of contentment, but they are both keen for it not to define them.

'In a building like this, it would be very easy for it to start defining us as people,' says Deborah. 'I think that's something that has to be overcome. Although it is our home, and something that we have created, we are not a tower! We are something completely different from it. I suppose what I'm trying to say is, are we interesting people because we live in a water tower, or are we interesting people that live in a water tower? Obviously, I'd prefer us to be the latter.'

The Long View

The story of this family is central to *Grand Designs* culture: a tale of a young family that included an architect, a ruin to restore and an adjacent new build that took its language from commercial buildings. Most importantly, their story has, in order to reach fully rounded maturity, included a hugely important architectural component: time. Something that is rare to be able to chronicle on television.

Andrew and Deborah's account of living in their home is as touching as it is real, and perhaps the most lingering reflection is how living in such an extraordinary assembly of spaces has had a lasting, positive impact on everyone who has lived there, especially the children.

The separate components of tower, house and garden seemed odd bedfellows when the home was first finished. Now they collaborate as entertaining players telling the story of one fabulous environment.

1999
—
Straw Bale House
—
Islington

•	Episode aired	1999
•	Location	North London
•	Owner(s)	Sarah and Jeremy
•	Architect(s)	Sarah Wigglesworth and Jeremy Till
•	Build cost	approx. £1 million over three contracts (as of 2024)

As one of the first homes to be featured on *Grand Designs*, architects Sarah and Jeremy's 'straw bale house' is really a tale of two beginnings. For Sarah, who was then in her late thirties, this was the first building she had designed from scratch. 'The scale of it and the combination of high and low technologies made it incredibly demanding,' she says. 'We were breaking new ground.'

At the same time, the *Grand Designs* team were breaking new ground – albeit less literally. It soon became apparent that Sarah and Jeremy's self-build schedule would not bend to the filming schedule. 'After two years on site, we moved into a watertight building, but it wasn't completely finished for another two years,' says Sarah. Hence, our concept of the *Grand Designs* revisit was born.

An amalgam of experimental ideas and materials including straw bales, gabion piers, sound-nullifying sandbags and sheets of pillowy silicone-faced fibreglass, this eco-build baffled some critics. 'It just didn't go down very well,' Sarah says. 'Architecture can take itself quite seriously and I think they found it wilful and overly playful. As a studio, we only ever built one other house and I think that says quite a lot. It definitely was not a pot of gold ...'

Their large, L-shaped building was conceived as a live–work space, with Sarah's architectural practice, SWA, occupying one wing of the building. (Their 'private world' can be accessed via a dining/

conference room that acts as a mediating space between the two.) Over 20 years, SWA has gained international recognition for its public buildings, including social housing, schools and community centres, but Sarah's home remains her 'biggest visiting card'. 'In a way it acted like a piece of art,' Sarah says. 'It burst upon the scene and made everyone question their own assumptions, and that's quite unusual for architecture.'

Gradually, the architectural world appears to have caught up with the prescient ideas explored at the end of what is a short, quiet residential street in North London. 'Low environmental impact, recycled waste and low-embodied energy are all ideas that this building wears on its sleeve,' Sarah says. 'These are all now very prominent ideas in the conversation about what architecture should be doing, and actually, I do take a little bit of credit for that.'

During filming, Sarah described the project as 'something of a plaything for us architects ... You can test an idea on paper, but the proof of the thing is in the building of it, and the experiencing of it and the living of that life.' Now, having lived in their straw bale house for over 20 years, she is 'quite surprised how much we got right'.

Since designing the Straw Bale House, building regulations have changed and sustainable technologies have evolved. In 2017, Sarah and Jeremy enlisted the help of a company to analyse

the energy efficiency of the building and a 'spatial and environmental upgrade' ensued. Over nine months, warped timber window frames and a leaky section of roof were replaced. Any unregulated air loss through the fabric of the building was plugged. 'We've worked out that we've saved 62 per cent of our carbon which is amazing,' Sarah says.

The couple also took the decision to age-proof their home at the same time. 'We knew we wanted to stay here and that it would have to work for us,' says Sarah. They introduced level thresholds and handrails in the bathrooms, switched from gas to an induction hob in the kitchen and decommissioned the composting toilet to create space for a self-contained annexe on the ground floor, which could provide accommodation for a carer should the need arise. Their five-storey tower – a book-lined creative 'eyrie' – will keep them active in mind and body for years to come.

'Like an overcoat, a building mediates between you and the outside world and gives you pleasure,' says Sarah. 'That is what home is: a place where you feel most comfortable, that nurtures your soul – and a place where you can be your authentic self. I think often architecture is seen as just a neutral background, and I absolutely don't think it is. It's actually a live thing that you relate to. It changes you as much as you change it.'

The Long View

Twenty-four years since Jeremy and Sarah completed their home next to a mainline railway, the house seems almost timeless. Amid the jocular stories of its construction and the playfulness of the design lies a long-sighted yearning; the building both reaches back in a twentieth-century tradition of heart-on-sleeve organic construction, and points forward to a building language for this century. This sense of timelessness makes the place very interesting and I feel lucky that we were able to film it.

So it is not surprising that this house has had a wide-reaching effect on other architects' work, at home and abroad. It continues to be published and it's the single subject of a hefty tome that centres on Sarah's architectural practice that she continues to run from the studio in the building.

1999

—

Hedgehog Co-operative

—

Brighton

•	Episode aired	1999
•	Location	East Sussex
•	Owner(s)	Residents of Hedgehog Co-operative
•	Architect(s)	Robin Hillier/Bob Hayes/Jonathan Hines of Architype
•	Build cost	£60,000 per household (as of 1999)

The Hedgehog Housing Co-operative in the first series of *Grand Designs* was unusual: 10 households, all from the social housing list and in urgent need of accommodation, who signed up to build their own and each others' homes on a collaborative scheme just outside Brighton. The project was driven by Brighton Council and the South London Family Housing Association for whom the 10 were to be tenant-occupiers. The deal was that in constructing the homes they would earn 'sweat equity', trading their efforts and skills acquired along the way for reduced rents and a secured tenancy. It was – and remains – the ultimate model of building democracy.

This was a golden and rare opportunity, not because of the attractiveness of the deal but because the deal existed at all. There are other similar and wonderful schemes around the UK, some using the same design and construction process; there are private community self-build projects and inspiring co-housing estates; there are exemplary developer-led models where architectural ambition serves the needs of social housing. But these are all in the small minority. Generally, the more complex the arrangement of parts in housing, whether in the social or private sector, the more likely it is that a scheme will fail. And when a project demands the hard physical input of people who do not already enjoy a fully economically comfortable or secure lifestyle, the risk of it stalling or failing increases. So the opportunity of Hedgehog lay in the fragile collaboration itself, in the remarkable sustaining contract between council, housing association and tenants. No-one dropped out to threaten the viability of the scheme.

As to the design and construction, the team turned to an already-proven system evolved by the eminent architect Walter Segal. This involved a simple 'stick-built' approach of using readily available timber and standard sheets of board that anyone could learn how to handle. The Segal method had proved successful in a similar Lewisham scheme and it was reinterpreted at Hedgehog by two Segal disciples, the architect Robin Hillier and the project manager Geoff Stow.

We returned with the cameras in 2012 to see how the project had fared over 13 years, and the results were astounding. The buildings had settled into a prickly coat of foliage and orchard; a community shed, beehive and work spaces dotted the shared gardening areas. The 10 original families were all still there, making in one form or another, some kind of social contribution, for the simple reason that the reduced rent they had enjoyed had created time and space in their lives to give something back to the community. Sweat equity had created long term social capital.

The only tangible sadness of this scheme was that we were not able to find more like it. It felt ironic that in our first flush of filming, we had chanced upon a rare opportunity to record a community project that has not been repeated. But Hedgehog still holds the most powerful message of all the projects we've covered over 25 years, because it incontrovertibly proves that the core architectural process – of creating homes with your own hands and learning the skills of building – can empower and self-actualise people from all walks of life and with whatever means, in remarkable ways.

2001
—
Cruciform
—
Lambourn

•	Episode aired	2001
•	Location	Berkshire
•	Owner(s)	Rupert and Julie
•	Architect(s)	Hugh McCann of Roderick James Architects LLP
•	Build cost	£350,000 (as of 2001)

Rupert was on his way home from a kids' party when he first saw the plot of land he would build his family home on. He was local to the area and so knew the promise of the plot, which sat overlooking the Lambourn Valley in the North Wessex Downs – a protected patchwork of steep chalky scarps and soft rolling hills. His architect was less convinced, and had to stand up on the roof of his car to see the appeal. 'The view was completely obscured by a collection of large, ramshackle outbuildings and overgrown vegetation,' says Rupert. 'But once he was on the roof, he said: "I can see it: we can build something great here."'

In 1999, Rupert, his then wife, Julie, and their two young children, moved into the existing – rapidly deteriorating – bungalow for the duration of the build. 'That was hard,' Rupert recalls. 'The roof leaked, and the tiles were literally dropping off the bathroom walls.' Meanwhile, their new home had started to take shape about 15cm (6in) from their temporary accommodation. 'When you're seeing this lovely place being built right next to you, it did become more and more frustrating,' Rupert admits. The old house was swiftly demolished the day after they moved in next door.

Conceived as a green oak-framed, cross-shaped house with windows on every wall, the building reached out into the landscape, pulling in panoramic views of the valley. 'Those enormous views were such a strong part of the whole experience,' says Rupert. 'It wasn't just the isolated property – it was living on the top of the hill and watching the weather roll up the valley. That really is my abiding memory of the house.'

Rupert describes the build as 'plain-sailing – I'll do another one yet!' The spectacular green oak frame was crafted from 85 oak trees and assembled on site in just seven days. In that time, the four wings of the cruciform were perfectly aligned with the octagonal ring at the centre of the house before the roof was fitted, locking the structure together. 'The completion of the frame was a really big deal for the craftspeople who are so clearly passionate about what they do,' he explains. 'When the frame was finished, it was topped out with a sprig of oak, which was quite a spiritual moment.'

Life inside their oak-framed home was noisy, initially. 'The green oak made the most awful creaks,' says Rupert. 'Sometimes, you'd hear a huge crack in the middle of the night which certainly alarmed some of the people who came to stay during those first couple of years.' Rupert had been forewarned that as the oak aged, it would crack and twist before eventually settling down.

The noise of the ageing frame was accompanied by squeals of delight from the children, who treated their new home like an adventure playground. 'They used to get their roller skates on and chase each other around the outside of the kitchen,' Rupert recalls.

'If they got a new bike for their birthday, they would just ride it around indoors. In fact, I think Felix even rode his motorbike around the kitchen once ...'

The escapades continued outdoors. Whenever it snowed, the children would take their sledges out into their field and use their quad bikes to tow them back up the hill. Winter inside the house was, Rupert admits, slightly draughty. 'Don't get me wrong, it was extremely well insulated but because the structure wasn't airtight there were draughts that let the heat out in the winter.' Underfloor heating and a hefty woodburner kept them snug. The building was deliberately designed to cope with the exposed site on which it sat, with courtyard gardens providing shelter from strong winds and generous roof overhangs keeping the interiors 'beautifully cool'.

Rupert lived under the great oak frame for 11 years before separating from his wife and selling the property. 'I still drive up along the bottom of the road and look up at it and think: we did that,' he admits. 'Part of the attraction of building in green oak is that you're building something quite ageless. If circumstances were different, I'd buy it back tomorrow.'

The Long View

The architectural firm for Rupert's house was Roderick James Architects LLP. Rod James's early design work was forged in sustainable construction (he was the first director of the Centre for Alternative Technology), but he also professes a love for the historic traditions of building. Several decades ago he set up Carpenter Oak, a timber framing business, to commercialise the learning about historic oak framing and jointing that had been gleaned through the conservation of ancient buildings in the twentieth century. In many ways, it is Rod's work and energy that has driven the revitalisation of traditional oak framing skills, and his designs for houses reflect that. We are lucky to have been able to film two of them.

Rupert's home, an early iteration, showcases many traditional timber jointing techniques, but Rod and his team also introduced contemporary spatial ideas, modern ergonomics and many technical innovations into the building that bring oak framing into the sustainable age: he recounted to me how he had developed a simple and brilliant airtight technique to marry large triple-glazed windows with a building that will always want to twist and creak a little. Rod's influence is widely felt and his inspiring work has led to a new tradition of oak framing in the UK and around the world.

2001
—
Barn Conversion
—
Devon

•	Episode aired	2001
•	Location	Devon
•	Owner(s)	Martin and Sue
•	Architect(s)	Adrian Slocombe
•	Build cost	£350,000 (as of 2021)

Four years ago, Martin sat in front of the stack of invoices he had collected over the duration of his self-build. There were 20 piles: one for each year of the project. What began as a necessary administrative task turned into an autobiographical account of the creation of his home. 'You could see the pattern of work in these piles,' says Martin. 'And even though there were literally hundreds of invoices, I could pretty much remember exactly what I did with all of the materials.'

The remarkable story of Martin's home is made all the more poignant by the recent death of his partner, Sue, who lived here with him for 24 years – and together elsewhere for 11 years before that. She is described as 'the driving force' behind so much of what was achieved here – not least the completion of the building after 20 years. 'Sue was a very early adopter of environmental building principles,' says Martin. 'She was definitely the motivation behind that.' Those who have seen the episode will remember the lengths Sue went to to ensure as little concrete as possible was poured into the ground beneath their crumbling barns. 'We would have ended up with an awful lot more concrete in the house than we did if she had not been quite so strong about it,' says Martin.

The couple arrived in Devon having spent three years partially restoring a French château. They were drawn by Martin's childhood holiday memories and the local town, where their two boys, then aged three and five, would attend school. The barns – an amalgamation of three stone and cob structures from the seventeenth to the nineteenth centuries – were in 'a shocking state'. 'There was some hesitation about the scope of work,' Martin admits, 'but there was a feeling that we'd landed. I think we joked about it taking 20 years when we first started,' he recalls. 'I don't think we realised that the joke was going to be on us!'

When the family moved into their rudimentary, albeit watertight, home in 2001, they shared one bedroom and got on with their lives. 'It was a 20-year project,' says Martin, 'but there was an awful lot else going on in that time.' Both he and Sue embedded themselves in the local community, pursuing their own creative and intellectual interests while maintaining full and varied careers – 'the building was just one part of that'.

At no point did the manual work required – which included everything from flooring and walling to plumbing, wiring, joinery and decorating – feel onerous. 'We were always positive about the whole thing,' says Martin. 'And I think part of the reason for that is that we never felt we weren't in control of the process. We found that there was a solution to every problem and putting those solutions into effect became the interesting part of the process.'

That's not to say that mistakes weren't made along the way. The staircase that connects the kitchen to the garage went through three iterations, and the central oak beam that holds up the front of the house would have benefited from a flitch plate to prevent the inevitable bowing. But these are minor quibbles: 'Maybe that beam needs to sag,' Martin reasons. 'Maybe that's part of its charm.'

For Sue, it was important that work on the house was complete, and Martin is thankful that they were eventually able to enjoy four years together in their completed, handmade home. Martin, too, is grateful that the hard work is over. He compares the end result to a well-worn glove or jacket: 'Something comfortable I feel connected with. It belongs around me, and I belong in it.'

Now that he lives alone, Martin divides his time between the open-plan living area and the generous office under the thatch of the cob barn. 'At 4,000ft^2 (372m^2), the house is too large for one person,' he admits. 'But I do circulate within the space, so it doesn't feel unfriendly in that sense.' In time, he hopes to share the space with like-minded people, perhaps eventually opening up his home for a series of creative retreats.

Martin's rare and deep connection with the materiality of this building has not skewed his perception of home. 'Although I really wouldn't want to leave it, I don't think the box in which you live is the most important thing in life,' he says. 'Fundamentally, you can be at home anywhere if you're at peace with yourself. Home is, I think, more about what you're doing and with whom you're doing it and the impact you're having on the world.'

The Long View

It was exciting in 2021 to revisit this project from our very first series. The restored barns had mellowed to an age where they warranted some light maintenance and upgrading. The apple trees, newly planted in time for the millennium, were a mature orchard. The boys had grown into men grateful for the experience of spending their lives in a building that has encouraged them to grow, experiment and learn.

Martin and his late partner, Sue, spent decades philosophically and intellectually enriching this home using craftsmanship, traditional building techniques and care. The most exciting addition to revisit was the new cool larder: part of the house yet thermally insulated from it and chilled by the earth to require no energy.

Perhaps the guiding spirit here was Sue, who left a thoughtful home that combines conservation and an ethos of sustainability that reflects its time. Her wisdom was encapsulated in one idea she mooted back in 1999: meditate on the things that in your life you already know make you happy – and then bring them together in one building.

2003
—
Rustic
—
Sussex

•	Episode aired	2003
•	Location	Sussex
•	Owner(s)	Ben
•	Architect(s)	John Rees
•	Build cost	£28,000 (as of 2003)

In 2002, woodsman Ben built his own home deep in a protected area of ancient woodland he has lived on and managed since 1992. It was built on a budget of £28,000 from renewable local resources: sweet chestnut beams, barley bales and lime plaster walls. The workforce was made up of volunteers who came from far and wide to share their skills and experience living in the woods for a while. 'The build was a joy,' says Ben. 'It was as though there was a carnival going on, and in the background, we put up a building ...'

Ben had lived under canvas and in temporary structures for a decade before he applied for permission to build a permanent dwelling on the site. Though the battle for planning was hard won, it gave Ben something no architect usually has: 'the luxury of time.' For years before building commenced, he lived in the exact location his house would be built on, observing the shifting seasons and meticulously planning what it was he needed.

The framework for Ben's house was made entirely from 30-year-old poles he had coppiced from a 300-year-old chestnut tree. Now, 22 years on, the cyclical and self-sustaining nature of that process is even more apparent: 'I can see the patch where I cut the poles for my house and know that, in eight years' time, I can go back and cut the exact same poles from the exact same tree I built my house from and build another house. When you compare that to

where we mainly source building materials from, it's a very different picture.'

The frame raise was a key moment in the build that would see Ben's finely wrought plans take physical shape. Relying largely on the strength and goodwill of volunteers (there were 96 in total), he admits the carefully choreographed manoeuvre was the result of some lucky guesswork. In fact, I'd add, luck played its part in the safe completion of Ben's woodland dwelling. When the time came to clad the roof in chestnut shakes, Ben wanted the volunteers to be 'roped on'. He recalls sitting around the campfire at breakfast trying to figure out how to safely proceed, when a fresh volunteer wandered towards them out of the woods. When Ben asked who he was and what he did, he was staggered by the response: 'I'm Tom and I'm a rock-climbing instructor.'

The carnival atmosphere carried Ben and his crew of volunteers through the seven-month build. For some, the experience was life changing. (One of the volunteers gave up his day job to specialise in building sustainable wooden structures.) For Ben, even the most rudimentary of home comforts had a profound effect: 'Just to have hot running water, light, warmth and a place to relax at the end of the day has probably extended my life by 10 years,' he says.

The transition from canvas to cosy cabin did take some getting used to, however. 'I hadn't really lived in anything with proper walls for about 10 years,

so when I first moved in – although I did love the quiet and the stillness – I also felt slightly disconnected from the woods,' Ben says. To this day, he sleeps with a window open above his head.

Ben has three children. When they were younger, he built them each a bedroom from the same self-sustaining materials. 'That was satisfying because I was able to construct the extra rooms as a completely separate building,' he says. 'Then, once it was finished, I got the chainsaw and cut out the connecting straw bale to create the link between the extension and the house.' Other than that, very little has changed inside his hard-wearing home. 'I bring a wheelbarrow of logs into the kitchen every morning to keep the Rayburn going,' he explains. 'This place was built to deal with what is a fairly rugged way of life. Ultimately, you create the space you need.'

The impact of Ben's woodland dwelling was far-reaching. Over the following decade, his work segued from forestry into building. He's particularly proud of the community shop he built: 'A lovely example of a roundwood timber frame building right in the heart of our village.' Nowadays, Ben has been able to refocus his attention on the forest. 'I can confidently say that I know this bit of woodland better than any other human being on the planet,' he says. 'I'll be totally honest,' he continues, 'as much as I love the house, I do see it as a product of the forest. It's the forest I really love.'

The Long View

For nearly two decades, Ben's woodland project has been one of our viewers' favourite films. Nothing goes wrong, there is no overspend and the resulting building seemed to be without compromise. This proved to us that it is possible to make compelling television without relying on the now-tired editorial notion of 'jeopardy'. It also proved that it is possible to make a serious film about sustainable construction and the global issues it throws up (around resource use, recycling and embodied carbon) without lecturing to our audience. If memory serves, the word 'sustainable' crops up infrequently, usually from Ben's mouth.

To deploy a much-used *Grand Designs* term, both the project and the film had 'integrity'. The incidental music even came from the location filming: one of Ben's many helpers was the musician Mike Fry, whose minstreling accompanied the raising of the round-pole cruck timber frame. Fry's principal role was to go shopping for the team's daily food, and he excused himself from carpentry – he rightly valued his guitar-plucking fingers.

2003
—
Waterworks
—
Chesterfield

•	Episode aired	2003
•	Location	Derbyshire
•	Owner(s)	Leanne and Chris
•	Design	Leanne and Chris
•	Build cost	approx. £150,000 (as of 2003)

Our relationship with our heritage can be fraught, especially when we stray from the path of convention. Whereas we can, with the passage of time, recognise the value of a Victorian house or a polite Georgian street, we have greater difficulty in calculating the value of a Victorian sewage pumping station or an Edwardian railway signal box. The truth is that value lies in the quality of a thing, its associations and its rarity. Note: there are not many signal boxes left to conserve.

This Water Board pumping works was such a thing: rare; well built (with an astonishing terrazzo floor that folded up the walls to deal with any flooding); and abandoned, a victim of modern pumping technologies that 20 years ago were leaving utility buildings like it redundant around the country. Today they've all been converted into Airbnbs.

Leanne and Chris, with very little help, felt able to take on this leviathan of a building 20 years ago. They were early pioneers of the vintage movement, exploring steampunk before it became fashionable and selling vinyl records by post before analogue hipsters were invented. This approach, leaning towards keeping as much of the building as possible and respecting its structure, led to a remarkably sympathetic adaptation of the place. It was conservation by another name with an extra 30 per cent of imagination.

Meanwhile the film was an opportunity for us to explore the history of utility buildings. Water and sewage pumping hadn't exactly forged its architectural identity in the nineteenth century – utility buildings at that time were tricked up to resemble cathedrals, banks, country houses and temples. Then, with the widespread distribution of electricity, came the need for a design approach on a new and epic scale. Giles Gilbert Scott evolved his massive, simplified 'power station' style for the London Power Company in the early 1930s, producing austere and brooding Art Deco behemoths like Battersea and Bankside power stations.

Mercifully, his designs then influenced the architecture of all utility buildings across the country, including Leanne and Chris's building. Their pumping works is consequently in a 'Battersea light' style, built elegantly in brick and on a near-human scale.

2004
—
Beach House
—
Hastings

•	Episode aired	2004
•	Location	East Sussex
•	Owner(s)	Tom and Darron (current owner Marc)
•	Design	Michael D. Hall Building Design Services Ltd
•	Build cost	£350,000 (as of 2004)

At the age of 53, the self-described pop Svengali, Tom, was ready to 'throw down roots'. He had travelled the world managing bands such as the Pet Shop Boys, Bros and East 17, but his recent diabetes diagnosis had prompted a change of pace. With his partner of 11 years, Darron, Tom exchanged his hedonistic lifestyle for a patch of land on the East Sussex coast.

Initially, the duo refurbished a 1960s beachfront home, adapting it to their taste for 1980s Memphis-style design. 'I like Memphis because it's vulgar, crude, irreverent, playful,' Tom said at the time. 'It's Pop Art.' The couple's extensive collection of twentieth-century art and design – which included museum-worthy pieces by Philippe Starck and Andy Warhol – soon outgrew their Sixties/Memphis mash-up. When the opportunity arose to purchase a seaside shack two plots down, the couple began to imagine a more pared-back existence inside a Bauhaus-inspired beachfront behemoth.

Prior to working in the music industry, Tom studied at the London College of Furniture and worked as a designer for Terence Conran before founding his own design company. 'I've always wanted a white block of ice cream to live in – a white box to house our very busy, bizarre series of collections,' Tom explained to me during filming. Despite clamorous opposition from some locals, that is precisely what he got.

In June 2003 Tom introduced Bauhaus to a small hamlet outside Hastings. The house – a gleaming, three-storey building that towered above the neighbouring beachfront bungalows – was built in eight short months on a relatively modest budget. At the same time, the nearby Grade-I listed De La

Warr Pavilion was undergoing extensive restoration. Built in 1935, the Pavilion is widely cited as the first major Modernist public building in Britain. The seaside became the setting for some of Britain's finest Modernist buildings, including The Midland Hotel in Morecambe, Blackpool's Pleasure Beach and Brighton's Saltdean Lido.

Inspired by those pioneering, streamlined silhouettes, I described the house as 'a perfect little sugar lump' of a building. Constructed from hefty concrete blocks, UPVC windows and coated in an elastic white emulsion that could withstand relentless wind, sand and salt spray, it was designed to do the opposite of dissolving into the landscape. In fact, in 2006 Tom received the Sussex Heritage Trust Award. The award plaque has a prominent position on the front of the house.

Tom took complete ownership of the interiors, having worked with Conran on the design of numerous public interiors. The ground floor consisted of a garage, studio, photographic darkroom and stainless-steel kitchen with a 2m (7ft), bronze Dame Elisabeth Frink sculpture at one end. A library, master bedroom and guest bedroom (both with en-suites) and office were located on the first floor. The top floor was Tom's favourite space: a light-filled living room and gallery with far-reaching views of the minimalist seascape beyond.

Once the shell was complete, the intention was to rationalise their possessions, although Tom admitted they were having to 'fight themselves' to conform to this new, self-imposed discipline of minimalism. In addition to the contents of their existing home two doors down, the couple had a further three containers full of belongings to sift through. Darron was happy to approve the sale of his Steiff teddy collection, but the box of glass fish would be staying.

White-washed, starkly lit and clad in expensive flecked marble tiles, the interiors could easily have become anodyne, but the couple's curatorial eye for bright, shiny design objects transformed this house into a highly personal home. They had collected Memphis Group pieces for nearly a decade, and their top floor became a paean to Ettore Sottsass, the Italian architect and designer who founded the Group. 'His philosophy was: why do you have to put two materials together that match,' Tom had previously said. 'Why do all four table legs have to be the same? He [Sottsass] argues that conformity is laziness – that it's uncreative.' It was a philosophy Tom clearly adopted in his lifetime.

'This is my spiritual home,' Tom said when the building was complete. 'When I look out of that window, and I see that view I can't ever imagine living anywhere else.' Tom eventually separated from Darron, and continued living in the house with his partner and current owner Marc until his death in 2020 at the age of 70 – at home on the shifting shoreline, surrounded by his collection of non-conformist design.

The Long View

The most intriguing thing about Tom's home is how opinions about it have changed. When he built it, he faced significant local opposition. When she interviewed Tom in 2018 about his critics, *Grand Designs Magazine*'s correspondent Charlotte Luxford was met with a robust defence: 'I ignored them and referred them to my granted planning consent.'

Despite its nickname of the Sugar Cube, the building is remarkably historicist – reflecting Tom's connoisseurship – and seems to have sprung from the mind of Walter Gropius somewhere around 1925, as if it were a Bauhaus satellite building, a blank container for new forms of expression. That, plus a deft reference to the early Modernist architecture of Britain's coastline. In other words, it speaks of the erudition of its first owner (who trained as a designer). It was indeed built to contain his changing collection of contemporary art and his passion for 1980s post-Modern Memphis Group furniture and objects by Ettore Sottsass and friends. This isn't just a house; it's a physical landmark that attracts architectural pilgrims; and it's a cultural landmark too. Just what Tom wanted.

2004
—
Norwegian Longhouse
—
Glasgow

•	Episode aired	2004
•	Location	Argyll and Bute
•	Owner(s)	Jo and Tony
•	Architect(s)	Andy McAvoy
•	Build cost	£380,000 (as of 2006)

It is architecture's job not simply to provide shelter but to provide the conditions for people to flourish in a place, to look after them. And, as Daniel Libeskind has said, architecture is based not 'on concrete and steel and the elements of the soil. It's based on wonder'.

Jo and Tony understood this when they briefed their architect Andy McAvoy. They asked for an oak-framed house, one that would span medieval traditions and the twenty-first century for their site high up overlooking Loch Long on the Rosneath Peninsula, where the highlands meet the lowlands of Scotland. Andy's response was, in his words: 'A Viking typology not seen for a while ... designed so you can sit up as if you're in the hull of a ship sailing out to sea.' Employing the traditional curved crucks of ancient frames common to ships and to houses, 'it's meant to pay homage to the maritime tradition of the area and the curving oak beams are a historic reference to the ancient buildings of Argyll'.

The result was a striking building that referenced the ancient and the modern and provided Jo and Tony with a lookout post and a home hunkered into the hill. Sadly, it cost them more than they wanted. Jo described it as 'that rollercoaster feeling where you just want to get off'. Tony was incredulous: 'You get bills through the post all the time and just sit there and go "I can't pay this."' However, perseverance ultimately repaid them: 'At one point we did actually put it on the market just because things got so tough.' Tony mused: 'It was a balance as to what would make us happier, not having the debt or having the house. But we hung in and tightened the belt and got through that patch.'

The house repaid them with many happy years, although it suffered damage in the extreme storms of December 2012. It does sit in a very exposed position high above the loch, which both affords it extraordinary views and exposes it to the most demanding of weathers. It remains, however, a building based on wonder.

2005
—
Stealth House
—
Peckham

•	Episode aired	2005
•	Location	South East London
•	Owner(s)	Monty and Claire
•	Architect(s)	Richard Paxton/MOOArc/Flower Michelin
•	Build cost	£180,000 (as of 2006)

The story of Monty and Claire's 'Heath Robinson house' can be traced back to Monty's childhood. Growing up on a farm, Monty was happiest when 'making various things move'. When he came to London in his late twenties seeking work as an actor, Monty was introduced to the award-winning architect, Richard Paxton, who harnessed his inventiveness. It was while working for Richard that Monty began searching for his own plot of land to build on.

Monty's self-build journey began before he met Claire: 'I was young enough to naively believe it was possible, yet not so old that I was jaded and cynical. I suppose I had enough experience to know that, if I just kept going, it would get there – eventually …'

In total, it took four years for Monty to purchase an affordable plot on a narrow strip of wasteland between two nineteenth-century villas in Peckham, South East London. It took a further two years for him to convince the planners – and later, the bank – that his unconventional design for a single-storey, windowless house with moving parts could work, despite having the professional support of Richard, who effectively mentored Monty throughout the process.

'I definitely fell out of love with the building,' Monty says. 'Mainly because it was such a long, arduous process to start with. If I'd known the six or seven years of preparation that it needed, I'm not sure that I would have had the courage to start.'

Auspiciously, when digging the foundations, Monty heard the roar of Concorde's final flight and looked up to see its white vapour trails skimming across the sky above the site. From then on, his approach was to 'crack on and get it built as fast as I could'. The project had its low points: 'It was not a pleasant experience,' says Monty. 'It was quite relentless, and I was somewhat wired with the effort of it.' The filming days with us provided much-needed breathing space for Monty, who – with the help of a couple of close friends – was doing much of the physical labour himself.

During the build, Monty and Claire announced they were having their first child together. Their son, Flint, was three months old when they moved in in the summer of 2005. Initially, both Claire and Monty struggled to believe the building was theirs. 'When we first moved in, it was as though I was waiting for

the real owners to come home,' Claire recalls. 'It took about 18 months before I realised we could actually stay here.' Monty was similarly unsettled: 'It had been so difficult to buy and to finance, somehow there was always this expectation that it would be taken away from us.' It wasn't until the house was remortgaged and the building regulations were signed off that they began to relax in the space.

After nearly two decades, the couple now think of the house as 'an ongoing gift'. The main living space – with its one-of-a-kind retractable roof – has proved endlessly adaptable. 'Every inch of the house has been used in different ways, in different times,' says Monty. Parties, tango lessons, movie nights, sleepovers and lockdown exercise classes have all been held here under the constantly changing sky. 'It's a very alive room,' says Claire.

The bespoke ingenuity of the house – with its hidden toilet, secret spy hole, bath under the bed and sliding sink – continues to fascinate. 'People still queue up to see the house,' says Monty, who has welcomed architecture enthusiasts into his home since its completion. 'Having the opportunity to experience these spaces is exactly what inspired me 30 years ago,' he says. Claire, on the other hand, is simply grateful that she lives with someone who understands the inner workings of the building: 'It's a little bit complicated and unusual because it has sprung from Monty's mind, which is a hive of activity and creativity. As long as he's around, he can continue to look after it …'

Last year Flint left home for university, causing his parents to rethink the generous space they have. 'It might take another form now he's gone, but we're still enjoying the result of all our efforts,' Monty reflects. 'I suppose that's what's stopping us from doing it all over again.' Though he may never be ready to start another project from scratch, his advice to anyone contemplating their own build is clear: 'Feel the fear and do it anyway,' says Monty. 'It will pay you back tenfold.'

The Long View

Monty is a renaissance man: motorcyclist, actor, engineer and self-builder. He was never going to build himself a conventional home if he could help it, and his 'stealth' house is as maverick, surprising and as eloquent as the man and his family.

The house remains an eccentric and wonderful contribution to this part of London, but it also marks a collaboration between Monty and others around him, not least the late Richard Paxton, an architect of extraordinary energy and a matching maverick nature.

Richard died a short while after helping Monty complete his home, a building which exemplified many of Richard's talents, not least his understanding of enclosure, that walls don't exist to support roofs but to provide shelter and comfort. He understood the great Corbusian truth, that the business of architecture is to create relationships: with a building, with people and with the world at large.

2005

—

White House on a Hill

—

Belfast

•	Episode aired	2005
•	Location	County Antrim
•	Owner(s)	Thomas and Dervla
•	Architect(s)	Thomas O'Hare
•	Build cost	approx. £350,000 (as of 2009)

I've been travelling to Belfast for work and for play since the early 1980s, a time when sectarian violence exercised an angry grip on day-to-day life there. A typical city-centre recollection is of British army patrols policing relatively empty streets of barricaded shops. Today that city is long demilitarised and is as thriving and energised as any on the UK mainland. More so, perhaps. After the Good Friday Agreement of 1998, the convenient normalities of twentieth-century mainland life flourished across Northern Ireland – everyday things like motorway service stations, national supermarkets and restaurants. But cultural life has also hungrily raced to catch up and even overtake the experiences we enjoy in other parts of our country.

Architecture is no exception. *Grand Designs'* sister programme *House of the Year* has been a regular visitor and after several successive years of looking around homes in the province (including a fabulous win for Kieran McGonigle of McGonigle McGrath Architects in 2019), we roughly calculated that per head of population, in terms of award-winning projects Northern Ireland punches seven times above its own weight.

So, in looking back 20 years, Thomas and Dervla's project (finished in 2005) now seems to speak of the fast evolutionary catch up of the place, not least because the site they bought already had a tired and uninspired home from the 1970s stuck right next to a main road. In the spirit of the times, this young couple dared to chalenge what was possible, demolishing the old house and half a hill to form an assertive terraced new home that was almost wilful in its defiance of both conventionality and of the laws of nature. It held up the hill and provided comfort and joy where there had been none. It now seems as if this house embodied the young, unleashed energy of Belfast in those years, an energy which remains undimmed and is addictive for any visitor who cares to sample it.

2006
—
Cedar-clad Box
—
Stirling

•	Episode aired	2006
•	Location	Stirling
•	Owner(s)	Theo and Elaine
•	Architect(s)	Christopher Platt and Helen Campbell of Studio KAP
•	Build cost	approx. £390,000 (as of 2024)

Theo and Elaine have always lived peripatetic lives. Their work has taken them across the globe from Africa to the Baltics, via Europe and Scandinavia. In total, Elaine has calculated that they have lived in more than 30 properties, 'picking up ideas along the way'.

In 2005, the couple decided to put down roots in Elaine's native Scotland. They purchased a hillside plot with expansive views over the bristling Campsie Fells and took their scrapbook of international ideas to local architects, Christopher Platt and Helen Campbell. It was the beginning of a creative and collaborative process that ultimately resulted in the creation of a secure, adaptable space that has had a singular pull over this otherwise nomadic family.

'When we spoke to the architects about the project, they made a model of the hillside and showed us examples of the shapes of houses they thought could sit there,' Elaine recalls. 'One of the models was a cube like this, and I remember at the time thinking how horrible it was.' Elaine envisaged a white rendered cube structure but was reassured their building would be 'far more interesting'.

The 'box' was built above a concrete basement and clad in Canadian cedar which has slowly silvered and settled into the hillside. Theo admits that initially their home was 'a bit Marmite'. Villagers were unafraid to express their views on Theo and Elaine's new eco-home. 'Some people thought it was absolutely wonderful, some people thought it was absolutely horrendous,' Theo says. Over the years, however, it has 'become part of the village'. Elaine recalls a female cyclist passing by and commenting on the build: 'She was a retired architect, and she called our home "the hedgehog house". I invited her in for cups of tea whenever she was passing because she just enjoyed being here.'

Inside, the layout has been designed to maximise the sense of space, with generous windows that connect the building to the landscape and a double-height ceiling in the living area. A covered balcony off the dining area is an idea borrowed from a house they rented in Malawi; the triple-glazed windows and outward opening doors are weather-proofing solutions borrowed from Sweden. The heat recovery system has functioned faultlessly for two decades. 'The house remains the same temperature all year round,' Theo explains. 'In fact, we hardly ever

light the woodburner. When we do, we have to open the windows because the house is so well insulated.'

The couple spent 10 per cent over their £350,000 budget, which meant they had to do all the finishing themselves, which included installing three bathrooms. 'We learnt how to plumb and tile ourselves,' says Theo. 'If you look now, you can see our learning journey: the plumbing and tiling downstairs is acceptable, but you can definitely see it improve the further up the house you travel.'

After three years of living in their home, the couple and their two young boys moved to Cornwall and the Isles of Scilly, renting out their home to a succession of tenants. They returned over a decade later during the pandemic. 'We were actually amazed how well the house had been looked after,' Theo remarks. 'If you rent something out, you expect there to be issues with it when you return, but that wasn't the case.' Aside from kitchen appliances, nothing has been changed or replaced. 'I think that's partly because it was a quality build, and partly because it's such a nice place to be in,' says Theo. 'People are slightly more careful than they would ordinarily be.'

The house has obligingly adapted to their changing needs. During Covid, with their grown-up sons working abroad, the couple altered the function of some of the bedrooms. Both had private office spaces they could retreat to. 'It was very easy for us to create a routine and separation during lockdown,' says Theo. 'Elaine went one way, I went the other, and we met up again at 12.30 pm for lunch.'

Recently their son Timo brought six friends back home with him from the Netherlands for a weekend of walking in the hills. 'They were all six foot five or taller!' laughs Elaine, who remains forever grateful for their double-height space. 'I suppose I feel quite proud of it,' she reflects. 'We've always been very comfortable here and we've never felt like it wasn't our home, even though other people have lived here in the meantime. It will always feel like our place.'

The Long View

Theo and Elaine had travelled the world working in sustainability and healthcare. When they decided to settle in Elaine's native Scotland, it is hardly surprising that they weren't interested in a conventional home. Theo's father had built his own home, so he should too, and build it to be sustainable to boot!

Studio KAP designed them a mainly timber panel home using European methods of construction. The structure was prefabricated off site and is sheathed in wooden shingles. Nearly 20 years later, the house is as fine as it has ever been.

A beautiful container came ready-packed with a host of architectural experiences: a covered porch – a satisfying liminal space that provides shelter and an elevated platform; the hallway squeezes you, preparing you for expansive decompression as you walk into the apparently voluminous living space. This is semi-open plan but also (cleverly) semi-open section, so you can engage with the space around you and beyond to the hills outside.

You breathe easier thanks to the building's engineering. Mechanical ventilation and heat recovery deliver a constant supply of fresh air that is warmed by the extracted stale air. Studio KAP built Theo and Elaine a healthy home, one that is physically regenerative and spiritually renewing – and one that is good for the planet too.

2006
—
Water Tower
—
Ashford

•	Episode aired	2006
•	Location	Kent
•	Owner(s)	Denise and Bruno
•	Architect(s)	Derek Briscoe
•	Build cost	approx. £300,000 (as of 2006)

Denise and Bruno's story is as memorable as the design that the architect Derek Briscoe formulated for them. Denise was a furniture restorer and Bruno, an artist and teacher, worked with blind and partially sighted children. Their picturesque gamekeeper's cottage in Kent came with a strange concrete structure on legs, the naked engineering form of a water tower, designed by Edwin Lutyens before the First World War and intended to be dressed up with cladding (to resemble a traditional windmill in their region) but never completed. To this day it remains in its raw form.

The bare and weatherbeaten concrete was beautiful in Derek's eyes. He had busily worked through the late Seventies and early Eighties, enjoying the delights that Brutalism had to offer, and here was a ready-made skeleton not to clothe but to celebrate. Bruno describes being 'blown away' by Derek's design, which reinstated Lutyens' planned roof and slid a metal-clad series of boxes and tubes into the leg structure, clearly separating the new use from the old.

The building gave Denise and Bruno views over hills and trees. It gave them a stimulating home and free membership of the Architecture Club, a non-existent entity which delivers unexpected experiences and meetings when you commission an unusual building. In their case, they tell the story of waking one Sunday morning to find a bunch of Japanese nuns on an architectural study tour taking photos in their garden.

The house also gave these two aesthetes a remodelled identity – Bruno talked to me later of his gratitude for how the building had powerfully invigorated him. Denise, when I told her the pair of them were extraordinary, corrected me, saying: 'No, we're not extraordinary people; we're just ordinary people doing an extraordinary thing.' I remember that quote from 20 years ago because it cuts to the transformative core that *Grand Designs* tries to capture.

2007
—
Two Timber Houses
—
London

•	Episode aired	2007
•	Location	South East London
•	Owner(s)	Bill and Sarah
•	Architect(s)	Hampson Williams Architects
•	Build cost	approx. £800,000 (as of 2010)

The idea for Bill's brace of sustainable, self-built houses emerged in the rainforests of Aceh on the island of Sumatra. 'It was a pivotal time for me in my twenties,' Bill recalls. He was spending a month working for an orangutan rehabilitation centre. One morning, the owner of the centre took Bill on a trek through the jungle. 'He said: "I need to show you this," so we walked for about an hour to the top of this escarpment and we stood there looking out at this barren landscape that had been completely chain-logged. I realised then that if we didn't start using resources more carefully, we were going to be in trouble. That's where it started ...'

Through his furniture and joinery business, Ecoism, Bill has championed responsible sourcing for decades. In 2006, his self-build project became an inevitable extension of his commitment to living more sustainably: 'My wife Sarah told me, "If you don't do this, you're going to burst: just build it." And how good is that?' he asks. 'When you can actually exercise a desire like that? I'd recommend it to anyone.'

Bill demolished the carpentry workshop he had on a backfill site in South East London and spent the next year handcrafting two glass and timber eco-houses, the idea being that the sale of the second property would enable him to live mortgage-free in the other with Sarah, and their young daughter, Jasmine. But the final budget for the build 'went through the roof', escalating from £450,000 to almost £800,000. 'It was an all or nothing project,' Bill reflects. 'I knew I couldn't have a half-baked finish – the house demanded the finish that I was going to give it, so I had to beg, steal, borrow, create another contingency and just keep going.'

His own home was finished in the early hours before final filming took place. It took a further three months to finish the second property. 'It was quite difficult to get everyone remotivated if I'm honest, but we got it across the line eventually.' Of all the memorable moments during the build – including the particularly painful realisation that a typo on a measurement for a pane of glass would cost him upwards of £2,000 – moving in day remains the most significant: 'I'd spent another day on site, then I realised I wasn't going home because this was my home.'

The transition from building site to home 'was pretty well instant' for Bill. The family spent the following seven years tucked away in their 'urban oasis' surrounded by 26 other houses 'that you didn't even know were there'. Crafted from glass and cedar, and cleverly orientated to maximise natural light and minimise awareness of the crowded urban plot, the atmosphere Bill had created was uniquely clean and serene. 'It was a beautiful house to live in,' he says. 'We had very natural surroundings and a constant connection between outdoor and indoor. Weirdly, after a weekend at home, you'd emerge on to the street on a Monday morning and remember that we actually lived on a terraced road in London.'

From the steel pin foundations to the breathable lime paintwork, Bill's pursuit of sustainable building methods and materials was unwavering. At a time when green technologies were only just emerging, solar heating, LED lighting, green roofs and rainwater harvesting were all integral to Bill's perceived success of the project. 'If just one person saw the project and decided to build greener, then it was a success as far as I was concerned,' he says. Bill's belief in a sustainable future – coupled with the exquisite design and craftsmanship of the buildings – endures to this day, with both buildings being described as among London's most celebrated homes.

The family relocated to a converted barn in Cornwall in 2014. For Bill, it was a natural progression. 'There was no way I was going to be able to live in a traditional terraced or detached house again: I don't think I would have been able to move anywhere else.' He describes moving out as 'pretty emotional – until you drive away. In the end, you're a custodian, aren't you?' he reasons. 'It was nice to be able to pass it on.'

For Bill, home is a personal sanctuary: 'A place to kick off your shoes; a place to just be in your own space with your own people and surround yourself with a bit of love.' For Bill, that love extends through and beyond the fabric of the building to the wider world. After all, 'If we all do a little bit, it'll end up being a lot, won't it?'

The Long View

Each of Bill's houses is one of those eco-homes that follows the lightweight route: it is a super-insulated timber frame with a relatively low thermal mass (the ability to slowly absorb and release heat), sitting on lightweight mini-piles screwed into the ground. This approach is a pretty cheap one – and therefore compelling – and uses materials with minimal environmental impact.

The houses may be lightweight but they are also light, thanks to inward-facing glazing courtyards which minimise overheating. They are also ingeniously ventilated, with shutters and openings that draw fresh air up and through the building from the cooling gardens below. This containerised use of plants and their evaporative cooling effect has been adopted in Middle Eastern buildings for millennia and it is exciting to see it adapted for timber construction.

Hampson Williams Architects produced an unusual but appropriately introspective and shy design for a significantly overlooked plot. We need more exquisitely crafted and modest architecture like this.

2007
—
Straw Bale Roundhouse
—
Cambridgeshire

•	Episode aired	2007
•	Location	Cambridgeshire
•	Owner(s)	Kelly and Masako
•	Design	Kelly and Masako
•	Build cost	£110,000 (as of 2008)

The prognosis was not too good. A house in the shape of a plant cell, stuck on stilts in the middle of a peat bog in Cambridgeshire. No design expertise was on hand, there was no professional team, not even any proper machinery. Add to this few drawings, little experience and not much money.

Yet the result was astounding. Kelly and Masako, both keen on biodynamic food growing and the management of land, built a house which, thanks to the unity of its construction and philosophy, was almost entirely beautiful. It didn't look marooned on its legs, it appeared to float across the fenland, a half-timbered hexagonal galleon-cum-miniature-Globe-Theatre waiting for the rising sea levels to flood East Anglia.

There was science behind the idea, the notion that a hexagonal house conformed to a universal design, one that is produced when circular cells meet, one that occurs again and again in nature, in leaf structures and honeycomb, snowflakes and turtle shells. A hexagon might therefore be the shape that brings us closest to nature.

When we returned in 2009, we discovered that the biodynamic garden had flourished, and food abounded. Kelly and Masako's edible hedgerows and willow fuel crops were in production, for carbon neutral heating and foodstuffs. The house had grown a pond and a veranda. It all seemed happily berthed in its field in Cambridgeshire.

Their approach and their building seem very alternative, but in truth are more closely allied to the ancient traditions of our species, of food growing and gathering, providing shelter and inspiration and working with the forces of nature rather than against them. So many facets of our modern world, from fossil fuel consumption to pollution, the desecration of biodiversity and the industrialisation of agriculture, have turned out to be terrifyingly destructive. Kelly and Masako's six-faceted home sets an example of how we can build and live in much greater harmony with the natural world.

2008
—
Lime Kiln House
—
Midlothian

•	Episode aired	2008
•	Location	Midlothian
•	Owner(s)	Richard and Pru
•	Architect(s)	Icosis
•	Build cost	£440,000 (as of 2024)

When Pru and Richard began building their house they were living next door – in a cottage they had recently finished renovating. The plot, which is tucked into the hills of an old lime cement quarry, was purchased in 2003, designed and built gradually over four years, and lived in happily for over a decade before being sold in 2018. Today, the couple have come full circle and moved back into the cottage.

'Stuff changes', says Richard. 'The original thinking for the cottage was that it might be for our son, Henry, who has learning disabilities. In fact, the cottage isn't appropriate for him and, two years after moving into the new house, my parents were both diagnosed with dementia. Instead of renting out the cottage, my parents moved in and we were lucky to live next door to them for seven years before they both died.'

This unique site has accommodated many of the unplanned changes in their lives. Perhaps that is in no small part due to the years of meticulous planning that went into creating the house. 'I had to take a year off work just to get planning permission,' Pru recalls. 'It was a real campaign that required the strength of a titan.' Once planning was eventually granted and Pru had negotiated the supply of water and electricity to the site, the pair spent a further year drawing up plans for their new home and interviewing 14 architects, before settling on the only one 'who didn't have pound signs rolling in his eyes'.

Their vision was set out in a 13-page document that articulated their practical, stylistic and philosophical ambition for the building. 'By the time we put the first spade into the ground, we were completely clear about what was going to happen and in what order,'

says Pru. 'We ended up exactly where we thought
we would in terms of the building and what we
wanted it to do for us,' Richard adds. 'We didn't
move a single socket or light fitting from the original
approved plans.'

Their overarching ambition was to carry out
their plan in a blame-free, cake-fuelled environment.
Pru recalls: 'If the builders finished what they said
they would do by the end of the week, I'd bake them
a fresh cake every Friday. That was my part of the
deal and it worked: everyone was very amiable,
and everyone worked terribly hard.' Home-baked
bribes aside, Pru and Richard stuck by the builder's
no-blame policy. 'He made it clear from the outset
that there is never any point in blaming anyone for
anything,' says Pru. 'If something went wrong, then
what we had to focus on was getting it right.'

This approach carried them through the inevitable 'traumas' such as the moment Pru unwrapped their bespoke kitchen worksurface crafted from Caithness stone, only to realise it was black and not white as expected. ('When I phoned up the company to complain they said, "Well, if you put it outside, in about 300 years it probably will be white."')

A more welcome surprise for Richard was the uplifting effect the completed building had on him: 'However stressful my day at work had been, whenever I came home, I would just open the door and relax.' Pru also felt this 'wonderful sense of calm' in the space, which she attributes to the abundant natural light and expansive view of the mercurial Midlothian countryside.

During their decade at the house, the interior remained unchanged. Richard's only regret is financial rather than spatial: 'If I'd fully appreciated from the beginning the direct relationship between square footage and cost, I would have made the entire building 10 per cent smaller, which would have saved us around £45,000. And actually – in a house that large – you wouldn't notice if the sitting room was 23-ft (7-m) long, rather than 25 (7.5m)!'

Outside, the couple spent three years sympathetically reshaping the immediate landscape: repointing the lime kilns, installing a pizza oven in one, and digging a swimming pond in their naturalistic garden.

Despite the many memories formed within the well-insulated walls of the house, the couple found it remarkably easy to sell the property in what was an (unsurprisingly) well-planned move that enabled Richard to retire. 'It's just a house,' he says. 'We live together, with each other. That's where our home is: it's with each other.'

The Long View

Big. That's the adjective to describe this project. Big ambition, big scale, big vision, big furniture, big landscape.

But everything on this project worked. And everything was in proportion. The internal layout was simple and in fact modest: there was no gym or cinema room or equivalent indulgence but there was plenty of investment in craftsmanship. The scale was, and remains, large but it needs to be in this part of the world where the setting is open and the views distant.

And the landscape therefore demanded that the building hunker down into the hill, knit itself into the wildflower planting around it and weave a relationship with the adjacent historic lime kilns. Which all happened.

The dialogue of this project was between building and place, and it spoke eloquently of how bright, clear and confident architecture can happily co-exist, not merely with manicured gardens, but with untamed nature and wilderness.

2008
—
Sugar Cube
—
Bristol

•	Episode aired	2008
•	Location	Bristol
•	Owner(s)	Martin and Katherine
•	Architect(s)	Martin Pease
•	Build cost	£350,000 (as of 2007)

The core tension that lies within White Box Syndrome hovers between the excoriating rigour of a home that's minimal and white both on the outside and inside – an almost colour-free place that suggests no-one lives here, let alone a family with dogs – and the architectural purity of the idea. On the one hand you can admire something built to such a demanding regime. On the other, can you live in something so perfect?

Well, this family certainly could. Churchill's well-worn quote that 'we shape our buildings; thereafter they shape us' applied here. Any architect will also understand the inherent tension in this phrase, between servicing a client's needs and reflecting how they like to live, and delivering a building which is also an expression of hope and desire. As architect, client, parent and partner, Martin knew he had to tread this knife-edge path of design, and the *Grand Designs* film of this build told the story of this design journey.

As a commercial architect, Martin seemingly without effort brought a sheen to this building, a glamorous finish and an image of professional cleanliness that companies want and that many homeowners wonder, longingly, why it is their homes don't have it. It's an unusual term for a building but this is quite a sexy house: high gloss and high class. Its uncompromising nature makes it very seductive.

But that is to miss the project's core ambition: to provide a game-changing home for a family. One that explores the fascinating territory of how buildings look after people, which is best expressed in another quote, this time from Philip Johnson, a New York architect who, like Martin, built offices for business clients. He said: 'All architecture is shelter, all great architecture is the design of space that contains, cuddles, exalts or stimulates the persons in that space.'

2009
—
Vaulted Arch House
—
Weald of Kent

•	Episode aired	2009
•	Location	Kent
•	Owner(s)	Richard and Sophie
•	Architect(s)	Richard Hawkes of HAWKES Architecture
•	Build cost	£500,000 (as of 2011)

The family home of Richard and Sophie, completed in 2009 in the Kent countryside, remains 'the most exciting thing' Richard has ever designed. Viewers may remember it as 'the one that fell down' – a reference to the dramatic moment during filming when a section of the clay timbrel arch collapsed on to the crash deck below – but for Richard and Sophie it is a 'staggeringly gorgeous' home that has more than stood the test of time.

As is often the case, their self-build project coincided with other seismic life events: the couple were expecting their first child, Sophie took voluntary redundancy and Richard set up his own architecture practice all while grappling with the demands of a building that bravely eschewed tried-and-tested construction methods and materials. Despite this, both remember the filming process with fondness: 'We've always said we'd do it again in a heartbeat,' says Richard.

Final filming took place in February, just days before the episode was due to air. 'We had all our friends around for the whole weekend before the crew turned up,' Sophie recalls. 'There were about 12 of us with rollers just emulsioning everything white.' Sophie remembers their seven-month-old, Oscar, being pushed along on the dolly track by the crew, 'having the time of his life'.

We visited again in 2011, but it is only now, 15 years after the build, that the couple feel their

home has reached its full potential. 'When the cameras were there for the original episode, they captured this big, bright orange arch soaring out of the ground, with no landscaping to speak of,' says Richard. 'The house was always in the foreground, looking very shiny and new and big and bold. Now, having bought some extra land and planted lots of trees, it's less prominent.'

The tiles (made from clay dug up from a pond just down the road) have weathered, the wood has silvered and the green roof (planted with slow-growing seeds from a local nature reserve) has flourished. 'There were times when I thought I might as well just put a sedum blanket over the top and be done with it,' admits Richard, 'but now rabbits run over the roof; lizards and mice live in the soil and kestrels use the top of the arch as a lookout post.' In time, it has evolved into what Richard and Sophie always imagined it could be: a beautiful home 'stitched into the landscape'.

Internally, the house has shape-shifted as the family's needs have evolved. The wall that separated the kitchen from the playroom has come down and they've been able to improve the spec of their kitchen cabinetry and worksurfaces. The addition of a laundry chute has also improved the efficiency of day-to-day chores: 'We used to throw dirty laundry over the stairs down into the hallway and then carry it through to the utility room,' says Richard. 'Now we

have a chute that takes it directly from the bathroom upstairs into a cupboard right next to the washing machine: honestly, it's just amazing!'

The couple have recently been granted planning permission to build a garage and an annexe on additional land they acquired in 2012. The annexe will house a bedroom, games room and small gym for their teenage children and overnight guests to expand into. 'Aesthetically, it will look quite different,' explains Sophie. 'Philosophically, it is definitely a continuation of our house.'

The energy performance of the house has exceeded expectations. The air quality contributes to a year-round sense of comfort and ease. 'Because of the heat recovery system and the amount of triple-glazing, we never get that sense of cabin fever, even during the winter months,' says Richard. The new annexe will demonstrate the evolution of green energy systems with long-wave infrared heating and new off-grid technologies incorporated into the design.

'We didn't set out to build something pioneering and ground-breaking for its own sake', Richard concludes. 'We never intended it to be anything more than a house with low running costs in this lovely location. So now, whenever I'm walking up through our garden in the evening and the arch is glowing, I can look at it and go: "Wow: we did that!"'

The Long View

It is fascinating to see how the language of green building has evolved over the past 25 years or so: from the hairy, airy, leaky architecture of stick and mud homes built with dubious permissions, to the highly regulated and codified buildings that Passivhaus certification brings. Alongside this shift, as sustainability has become mainstream, there has been a (myopic) change in focus from the ecology of buildings and place to the single issue of carbon reduction in use. This is a necessary – if crude – measure if as a nation we are to meet our zero carbon targets.

The very best pieces of architecture take carbon reduction seriously while not eschewing the wider issues of sustainability such as resource use, food, biodiversity, culture and learning. Richard and Sophie's house sets down an important marker for craftsmanship and building traditions too, which is what makes it so intelligent, so rich and so important.

2009
—
Apprentice Store
—
Somerset

•	Episode aired	2009
•	Location	Somerset
•	Owner(s)	Ian and Sophie
•	Architect(s)	Threefold Architects
•	Build cost	approx. £485,000 (as of 2009)

Working on an old building – one that might be listed, have a rare industrial value or be an archaeological site – is a balancing act. The old paper mill that Ian and Sophie bought in 2005 ticked all these boxes, and so what followed was the expected high-wire act with planners, conservationists, industrial historians and ecologists. There were the stunts and tricks along the way that all old buildings throw into your face to throw you off the wire. Here, the challenges included three buildings with changes of level to match; industrial heritage (the mill made Turner's watercolour paper); no foundations; and mounting costs.

The scale of interventions can range from doing nothing to an old place, leaving it to fall down (still an acceptable route in some conservation circles and a standard method for ancient monuments until recently) to the opposite extreme of knocking it down and rebuilding it from scratch. Both are much easier than the balanced route Ian and Sophie took; both are unimaginative and neither saves our heritage nor the carbon footprint of the built environment.

Mercifully, Ian and Sophie's own vision, coupled with the imagination of their architects, Threefold, produced a beautifully conserved set of buildings that are elegantly stitched together. The foundations are now secure, the lime pointing exquisite, the windows and doorways retained. Yet the house is also remarkably contemporised; it is open, light and spacious. The masterstroke is that the circulation through three buildings at three levels is now not just improved but transformed, thanks to the invention of a set of gantries, levels and staircases that weave continuously around and through one spine wall, like a ribbon, to always land you in the right place.

All testimony to the creative and interpretive role that passionate owners and their architects can play in reimagining the past.

2010
—
Recycled Bungalow
—
Isle of Wight

•	Episode aired	2010
•	Location	Isle of Wight
•	Owner(s)	Lincoln and Lisa
•	Design	Lincoln Miles and Lisa Traxler
•	Build cost	£225,000 (as of 2012)

When I asked Lincoln to share the enduring memories of his self-build on the Isle of Wight, his response is completely unexpected: 'Yoghurt, poo and relentless rain.' The yoghurt and cow dung he is referring to were 'abstractly applied' to corrugated sheets to encourage the gradual growth of moss and lichen – an ancient 'coating system that goes off in 20 years'. The rain just added to the experimental anarchy of this storybook site.

In 2007, Lincoln and his partner, artist Lisa, purchased a 1970s, mock-stone bungalow set in ancient woodland. They spent two years concocting an experimental design for the site. The new structures – which draw on Lincoln's admiration for mid-century Modernism – would be clad in experimental materials including burnt larch and yoghurt-coated corrugated fibre cement. The original bungalow would remain steadfastly in situ, its crazy-paved stone hearth a memento of the previous building and a signifier of the couple's wider, no-waste philosophy.

Despite the driving rain, the build went ahead at breakneck speed in spring 2009. 'Ridiculously, I tried to do it in six months,' says Lincoln. 'That didn't work.' Instead, it took nine months and just £225,000 to create a multi-functional home four times the size of the original bungalow. For Lincoln, it was nine months of 'architecture and fun'. 'If the project had turned out to be a bit lacklustre, the process might have been a bit rubbish. But it didn't: it's a great building, so the process becomes memorable because of the finished thing.'

Lincoln's design was conceived as four separate spaces designed to meet the individual needs of his family. The Seventies bungalow was reclad, reinsulated and remodelled to form a 'teenage pad' for Lisa's daughter, Ellie. A separate studio wing provided workspace for both Lincoln and Lisa. (They made sure they had to step outside to get to work: 'Everyone needs a commute.') A light-filled kitchen, dining and living space was designed as a place 'for everyone to meet in the middle', and a secluded bedroom tower nestled in the treetops was created for Lincoln and Lisa.

'That house represents what I'm about, really,' says Lincoln. The combination of light, volume, materials and the connection to its woodland setting have coalesced to create what he calls 'a breathing space for brain and soul'. 'Think about making your cup of coffee on a Sunday morning,' Lincoln says. 'If you enjoy that process and it gives you a sense of oxygen, then you know you're in a well-designed environment. If not – if your doors are in the wrong place, or your corridor is too tight – then that will suck the oxygen out of a space.'

After six years, the couple were lured away from their woodland retreat by an immense Second World War bunker with expansive views over the Channel. 'The process of construction is an eternal

flame of discovery,' says Lincoln. 'The amount of waste that was produced during the construction process irritated me.' Innovations, both material and technical, minimised the waste produced during the build of the bunker – 'But still not to the levels I'd like.'

The bunker was sold in 2023 and Lincoln and Lisa are currently living in an Edwardian rental, wondering if mycelium technology is the way forward – if, indeed, a third self-build is on the cards. ('Lisa would be deeply concerned by that idea,' admits Lincoln.) For now, Lincoln is happy to pass on his advice to other would-be self-builders: 'Firstly, have a word with yourself and ask: "Am I up for this journey? Am I the right person for this adventure?", because you do need staying power and resilience.' Then, there are the fundamentals to get right: 'Get a good architect; get a soil test so the groundworks and foundations are straightforward; find the right building team; do your research. Without all this, your build will cease to be an adventure. Ultimately,' he concludes, 'you've got to have a brain and loads of guts – and Brits do. So have a go!'

The Long View

How do we reimagine the past? Conservationists talk of needing to preserve the narrative of a place, of keeping the changes and the patina of use in our buildings obvious. Developers cite the need to erase buildings in pursuit of efficiency, profit and supposed regeneration.

Lincoln and Lisa's approach represented the best that an architect and an artist can conjure. Lincoln set fire to his larch cladding to scorch it; Lisa threw cow dung and yoghurt at their agricultural cement board cladding to encourage algae and moss. The finished new parts of the building played with vintage moments as a container for recycled 1950s switches, door handles and chairs.

And armed with the mental souvenirs and memories of living in their twentieth-century bungalow they wove a new architectural world, a creative reinterpretation and historical reimagining of their old home, conserved in parts, added to in others. Their riposte to the conservationists and the developers used two remarkable weapons: imagination and love.

2010
—
Passive House
—
Cotswolds

•	Episode aired	2010
•	Location	Gloucestershire
•	Owner(s)	Helen and Chris
•	Architect(s)	Seymour-Smith Architects
•	Build cost	£600,000 (as of 2010)

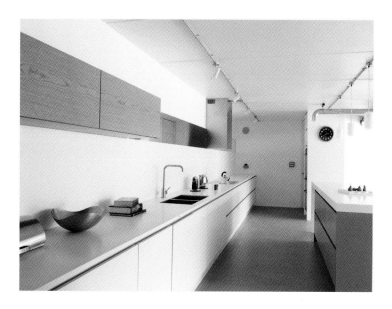

Architects Helen and Chris wanted to swap their small Georgian cottage in London for a home where they could 'see more sky'. So an underground house seems a surprising design choice, even if the location was a remote Cotswold hillside. Taking advantage of a rarely implemented piece of planning legislation that can allow buildings of outstanding architectural merit to be constructed in open countryside, they devised an ambitious scheme. Retaining the original crumbling barn above ground – a condition of planning permission – they would excavate a plot the size of two Olympic swimming pools underneath. And if that wasn't radical enough, they would build England's first accredited Passive House into the bargain.

Meeting rigorous Passivhaus standards (see page 247) requires an extremely high level of energy efficiency, meaning a building needs to be super-insulated and airtight. The design of this underground house involved using pre-cast concrete panels for the walls and the roof. The use of so much concrete might seem surprising for a sustainable building, but the panels were made using slag from blast furnaces which, as a waste product, has a much lighter carbon footprint than traditional cement. While the installation of the slabs was wonderfully swift, they required meticulous planning on Helen's part and complete precision in order to achieve the airtight standard needed and so avoid any need for heating. Triple-glazed windows and doors packed with insulation were other components, as well as tempered glass on the south-facing side of the roof which covered a kilometre of black rubber hosing, forming one giant solar panel.

Inside, for the three bedrooms and large open-plan kitchen/living/dining area, Helen and Chris chose a deliberately spare 'industrial' aesthetic with white-painted blocks on the walls, concrete flooring and exposed ducting. Helen described it as 'loft living underground'.

Their resulting house is totally invisible in the landscape above ground, with only the original barn standing as a signpost to what lies beneath. It's a fascinating outcome when such severely restrictive planning requirements in a conservative part of the world result in something as extreme and as radical as this build. Underground houses are notoriously difficult to construct, and when two people put a building together they so often compromise along the way. But here Helen and Chris shared the same passion and the same unswerving vision. The result? A building that reflects perfectly the will of its makers.

2011
—
Artists'
Barn
—
Braintree

•	Episode aired	2011
•	Location	Essex
•	Owner(s)	Ben and Freddie
•	Architect(s)	Anthony Hudson of Hudson Architects
•	Build cost	£980,000 (as of 2024)

When artists Freddie and Ben moved from their two bedroom flat in London into a sixteenth-century threshing barn in Essex 15 years ago, they received a handwritten card in the post. It was from an elderly gardener who had previously worked on the farm. He was familiar with the colossal timber structure, and he wrote to tell the new occupiers that he admired their achievement. 'I never met him, but the fact that he knew the barn previously and liked what we'd done just felt really good,' says Freddie.

Ben grew up on the farm, so to have the support of the local community helped in what became a gargantuan effort to lift this vast, 500-year-old, timber-framed structure from its slumber and turn it into a 'super-unconventional' home. 'It was a really rewarding experience,' says Ben of the self-build process. 'It pushed me beyond what I thought I was capable of.'

The 'gruelling' project took two-and-a-half years, with Ben working physically on site everyday for the duration of the build. The pair constantly wrestled with the scale of the undertaking and there came a point, a year into the build, when they assessed their progress and realised that they had essentially rebuilt the barn with insulation. It was warm and airtight but nowhere near complete: 'We thought we'd done the bulk of the work, but actually, that was the easy bit,' says Ben. 'We still had all the unbelievably painful detailed design work to do, to make the space habitable.'

When the time came to move their belongings into the barn, again, they were confronted by its inhuman scale: 'We put our daughter's bed into her room and it just looked ridiculous,' Freddie recalls. 'It was this tiny toddler's bed in this massive space, and it just felt really intimidating and unfriendly – until Ben built her a beautiful wooden bed that was more in keeping with the barn.'

Gradually, they adapted to the proportions of their new home while flatly refusing to 'niceify' their environment. They have filled the nearly 700m² (7,500ft²) space with their collection of ephemera, and abandoned plans to keep on top of cobwebs. The 8m (26ft) high wooden beams are impossible to reach without a cherry picker – 'And life's too short anyway,' says Freddie.

Outside, the landscape remains 'rigorous'. The working yard at the front of the building is bustling while the wildflower meadow they have planted at the rear is 'more wild than wildflower', though they are both thankful for the birds and mammals it attracts: barking muntjacs, barn owls and a bold swan who taps on the back door, waiting to be let in. They have since learnt that – true to its purpose – the threshing barn is deliberately orientated to channel the wind. Leaving either door open is problematic, even without the presence of the swan.

Since we first filmed Freddie and Ben, they have converted one of three corrugated iron grain silos at the front of the barn. During lockdown, Freddie held online lectures from here. Today, it functions as Ben's yoga studio. Apart from their daughter's bedroom, it is the only private space in the barn. Their own bedroom – and even the toilet – are not enclosed. ('Rule number one: don't go to the toilet if you're expecting anybody,' says Freddie.)

Freddie's advice for undertaking a self-build is characteristically direct: 'If you can't agree on simple domestic decisions, don't build, because there are so many decisions to be made, it's actually quite exhausting.' Their way around this was to limit their decision making by using materials that were already on site, including half-empty cans of paint left over from their London home and battered fixtures and fittings found in the barn. 'I like the fact that those things have been carried forward,' says Freddie.

Ben's advice is counterintuitively loose: 'Beyond getting planning permission, I really wouldn't bother doing any planning at all,' he suggests. 'If you're restoring a building, you never know what you're going to find when you start taking it apart.' The building will have a pace and momentum of its own: 'Once you've started, you can't stop. You just have to keep going, so be prepared for that.'

Freddie agrees: 'The building is in control: you're not. You have to accept that and go with it. In fact, that's the one thing that I feel really keenly about this barn: it doesn't care for us at all. We're just passing through. Its life is way more solid than ours and I think that's kind of fascinating.'

The Long View

Barns, like churches, don't convert easily. Their open nature defines what they are, so any slicing up of the space will lacerate the spirit of the place. Ben and Freddie knew the last thing they wanted to do was modernise their barn into cosiness. As artists, they wanted to retain the full-height monumentality of the ancient timber frame, preserve a view from one end to the other, and resist the idea of 'rooms'.

With the help of the visionary architect Anthony Hudson they externally insulated the frame and added ingenious insulated skylights to Anthony's design that remain invisible from outside. They added underfloor heating and repaired and conserved the ancient structure.

In fact, the entire project pushes at the boundaries of repair and conservation by replacing every trashed or useless component in the building with a brilliantly devised modern alternative. It also pushes at the boundaries of decoration – the home is furnished like a friendly museum (inspired by the Pitt Rivers Museum in Oxford), to house Ben and Freddie's vast collections of memorabilia, toys and stuffed animals. The result is a highly tuned and awe-inspiring live–work building; and it is hugely accomplished.

2011
—
House in the Hills
—
Herefordshire

•	Episode aired	2011
•	Location	Herefordshire
•	Owner(s)	Ed and Rowena
•	Architect(s)	Greg Noble
•	Build cost	Unknown

The architect Louis Kahn said that 'Architecture is the thoughtful making of spaces', the crafting of controlled volumes with careful, considered contemplation. The contemplation is part of the job description, a job which architects do 20 times faster than you or I could, thanks to the years of training they endured.

By deduction, the alternative to employing an architect and a builder is to craft your own space, but to let it take 20 times as long to allow the considered contemplation to happen. This more leisurely route is not common, but it chimes with the objectives of the Slow Movement, of which Ed and Rowena are devotees. For 23 years they have eked out a contemplative living on the eight acres (3 hectares) of hill they own in Herefordshire, tending to their animals and raising their children. As Ed observed: 'Our aim was for the land to produce food and wool, and we saw the house and land as one. A place to live the lifestyle we wanted for ourselves and our children … [a lifestyle that is] slow, sustainable, local, organic and whole'.

Ed, an estate manager, had worked on the restoration of the Joseph Paxton Conservatory at Hampton Court, where he met the architect Greg Noble. Greg produced the outline design for the home while he explored with Ed what a crafted, whole, slow-made house could be: 'Ed and I worked together rediscovering vernacular forms, craft skills and locally found materials'. The result is a wonderful home, made almost entirely by one man as a gift of love, care and craftsmanship to his family. It is the antithesis of the conventional recommended approach of 'finish the project, move in, start living your life'. Ed and Rowena lived for years with their children in a small annexe on the site that Ed had previously constructed as a trial exercise for the main house. It gave them space and time to take the long view and approach building more as a way of life. At some point they all moved out of the 'dugout' annexe and into the big house as Ed carefully continued to weave among them, adding to the building daily.

The process is ongoing, of course. Bedroom curtains on rails are replaced in turn by homemade doors in oiled timber, hung on Ed-made wooden hinges and closed with Ed-carved wooden latches. These details are worth waiting for, as the whole family appreciates. The building doesn't simply develop towards completion, it evolves like a living entity. Earth floors need to be occasionally rewaxed and polished, just as external window frames need occasional maintenance. This all gives lie to the fiction that buildings ever get finished: snagging works morph seamlessly into maintenance on any project.

The advantage here is that Ed and Rowena do not have to pretend they need perfection; they have no conceit of an artificial deadline; and, as hoped, the children, who are now adults in tertiary education or out in the world, seem entirely at one with this position. We have returned to film again and again; to see their eldest, Robert, build his own studio space on the land, to see Ed's mother move into her own Ed-built annexe, to find him busy on a neighbouring new home for his sister. And with every visit we are reminded that there is more than one way to design and build.

2012
—
Glass House
—
Brixton

•	Episode aired	2012
•	Location	South London
•	Owner(s)	Carl and Mary
•	Architect(s)	Carl Turner of Turner Works
•	Build cost	£600,000 (as of 2024)

In 2009, architect Carl and his partner, Mary, purchased a rundown house in Brixton. The plan was to parcel off the land, knock down the garage and build themselves a new home at the bottom of the garden. 'We started sketching out houses that didn't look that different to the Victorian terraces nearby,' Carl recalls. 'We were thinking, "What would be least offensive to the planners?"'

Unenthused by the plans that were emerging, they took a step back from the drawing board. 'It dawned on us that we might only get one chance to build our own house,' says Carl. 'I asked Mary, "If we could build anything, what would we build?" That was the beginning of Slip House.'

The house went on to win the Manser Medal, an award given to the best house in the UK, in 2013. It also became a game-changer for Carl's practice, eventually enabling him to move on from private residential work to larger public commissions. 'It's a project I'm really proud of,' he says. 'It was more successful than I could ever have imagined.'

Beyond the immediate Victorian terraces, Carl looked down the length of the road and identified 'a plethora of architectural styles,' including Art Deco houses, industrial buildings, a prison – even a windmill. A self-build eco-home had recently been built a few plots down, which enabled Carl to envision a terrace of individually designed sustainable houses. The challenge was to design a house that 'worked really well on its own as an object or sculpture, but that could eventually be subsumed into a terrace'.

What emerged was a stark, sculptural stack of three cantilevered boxes constructed from translucent glass panels. The ground floor was conceived as a large, adaptable workspace or self-contained flat.

Two bedrooms were located on the first floor, with the kitchen and living space on the light-filled top floor with a secluded roof terrace above. 'Mary's reference for the space was a monastery,' says Carl. 'It needed to be very minimal, very calm and restful.'

Fortunately, their planning officer supported the project from the outset, and they met with no objections from the locals. In 2011, their 'pipe dream' became a reality. 'We soon realised we didn't have enough money to build it,' says Carl, who also took the decision to build Slip House to the Code for Sustainable Homes – an exacting approach that came with 'huge hidden costs'. They sold their house at the other end of the garden and their barn in Norfolk, and took out a self-build mortgage to fund the build of their startling, see-through home.

Energised by the filming experience and Carl's vision for the site, it became a 'project built with love'. 'Everybody knew that it was going to be a really special house, and everybody raised their game,' says Carl. The groundworks were a slog, but seeing the outline of the building emerge in the form of its steel frame was 'super-exciting,' as was the arrival of the glass cladding panels, which slotted in with ease. 'We could immediately see what an impact the look of the building was going to have,' says Carl.

For Carl's studio, the house became 'a vehicle' through which to experiment with sustainable design and kit-of-parts architecture. 'We thought of it very much as a sort of prototype terraced house for the twenty-first century,' he says. In 2012, Carl moved his practice into the ground floor, while the top two floors became the couple's private home – a minimal urban sanctuary. 'We'd thrown everything at the house to make it what we wanted,' says Carl.

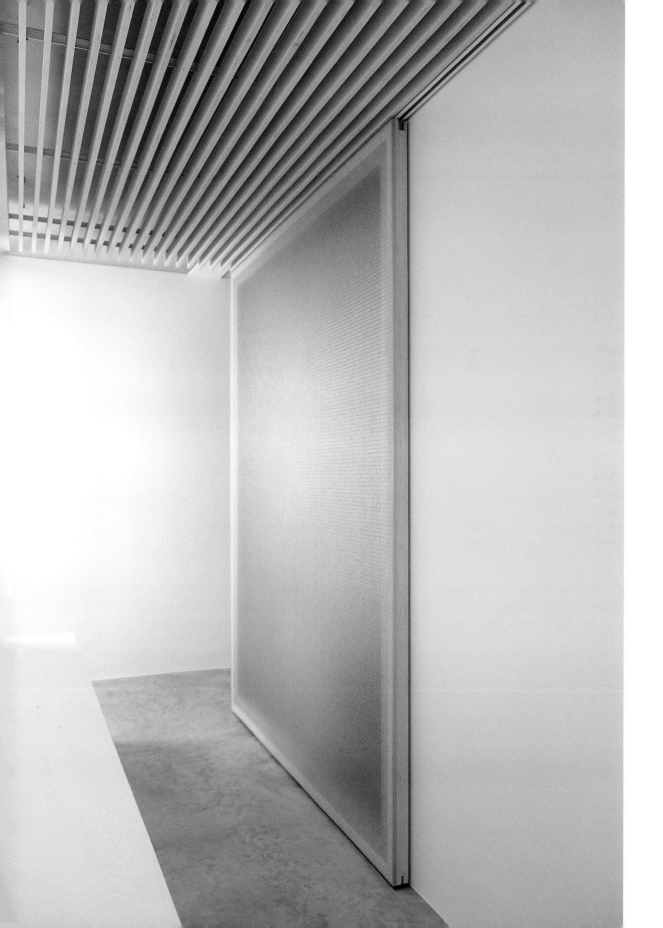

'Not just money, but time and energy too; we honestly had no intention of ever moving.'

But the house became a calling card for Carl's practice. Every time a client came to the studio, a house tour became inevitable. At times, Carl admits it felt as though they were 'living in a show home'. And, although they had hoped the project would generate public projects, in fact it led to two years of enquiries from private homeowners with awkward plots. Often, Carl's designs would get his clients past planning, only for the plots to be sold on for development.

When the opportunity to design Pop Brixton – 'a mini city of culture, enterprise and community' – arose, Carl realised he would need to sell the house to invest in the next stage of his career. It was a decision he didn't take lightly: 'On some level, it's still a regret because we'll never really be able to build another house like that,' he says. That said, the move has propelled him on to projects that have enabled him to explore the power of architecture beyond private homes. 'As I've matured, I think I worry less about what things look like and more about trying to empower people,' he says. 'If it's done well, I think architecture can be an incredibly inclusive, powerful, transformative thing.'

Mary and Carl remain 'serial renovators,' having created several homes since selling the house in 2014. Today, they divide their time between two renovation projects: one above a shop in Peckham, the other on the coast in West Sussex. Nowadays, home is less of 'a vehicle' and more of a place to 'bring up the drawbridge' and find stillness. Until the next project, at least.

The Long View

What does it take to build an award-winning home, one that scoops the Manser Medal – or the RIBA House of the Year, its successor – and goes on to take its place in the pantheon of global architecture, influencing other buildings and contributing to the discourse about climate change?

Carl's is one such home. It was built by him and his brother to house Carl and his wife, Mary, plus his architectural practice on the ground floor. It was built to be green: super-insulated with a high thermal mass, solar photovoltaics for electricity and a ground source heat pump, which could also work backwards to transfer excess heat from additional rooftop solar thermal panels.

But it didn't start out that way. Carl began by designing a modern take on a conventional terraced home with a pointy roof, with the option of a second adjacent home. 'But then we said "Let's forget the planning guidelines. Let's design the house we want and make the case for it."'

The result is a spectacular success, beloved by neighbours as much as by architecture critics.

2012
—
Artists' Muse
—
Skye

•	Episode aired	2012
•	Location	Isle of Skye, Inner Hebrides
•	Owner(s)	Indi and Rebecca
•	Architect(s)	Rural Design
•	Build cost	£150,000 (as of 2012)

When, aged 15, Indi visited the Findhorn Foundation, a Scottish sustainable community outside Inverness, she was profoundly inspired. Thirty years later, with her then partner, Rebecca, she finally found an opportunity to put into practice some of the ideas that had moved her, when the two artists found a scrap of land on the northernmost part of Skye. A site for the smallest of eco-homes with perhaps a studio, it was a perfect vantage point from which to watch sea eagles and whales.

The architecture of Skye was not, at that time, progressive. Traditional single-storey crofting cottages littered the countryside and, as they told me, Indi and Rebecca faced significant opposition to their plans – all of it, it has to be said, from non-resident owners who felt that the character of their holiday home island might be threatened by a modern building. The permanent residents on Skye were hugely supportive of the idea, instinctive in their knowledge that new architecture can be regenerative.

And in any case, the project and the design were carefully driven by Alan Dickson of Rural Design, a practice which had already designed a handful of highly contemporary buildings on Skye. So the island had precedent.

Alan's design took inspiration from the boulders that are strewn across the landscape of Skye's northern area. The result comprises two buildings – house and studio – each roughly diamond-shaped in plan with pitched turf-covered roofs, as if the boulders had grown a cap of moss. The external walls are clad in untreated larch that has now weathered to a stone colour but which, when fresh, still radiated that pinkish resinous colour that redwoods share. Alan described it as a 'bad fake tan' that would weather away. It has.

The design appears as adventurous and uncompromising as you would expect from two artists. But the chief governing factors for Alan were money and the weather. He knew he had to build an inexpensive small home that could withstand the terrifying winds of this part of the world. So, taking inspiration from the traditional stone-built black-houses on the island, he figured that a house without wide eaves, with a sculpted aerodynamic form and with a heavy roof would do the trick. The result is a timber-framed structure, discreetly reinforced with a small amount of steel, that supports an 18-ton earth roof. The cladding and the end wall of glazing to provide the sea views make up the walls.

The poetic result of this design, coupled with a modesty of scale, have had a powerful impact on the island. Tourists of all sorts stop to photograph the house and the architectural ones knock on the door. Alan's practice has flourished, and his work has contributed to a changing view in the Highlands and Islands of Scotland that contemporary rural architecture has an important interpretive role to play in our relationship with landscape – and an important regenerative role in rural economies as a vibrant statement of faith in a place.

2013
—
Flint Farm
—
Newbury

•	Episode aired	2013
•	Location	Berkshire
•	Owner(s)	Michael and Phil
•	Architect(s)	Sara Gardhouse of Taate
•	Build cost	approx. £800,000 (as of 2013)

Phil and Michael gave up their urban lifestyle and moved to a rural smallholding in Newbury, Berkshire in 2009. The plot they had purchased came with agricultural ties, which meant they needed to earn a living off the land. Undaunted, they immersed themselves in their new vocation, rearing rare breed animals and, later, running a successful brewery.

While working on the land, they often unearthed sculptural nodules of flint which they took back to their 'depressing' alpine-style farmhouse to admire. Two years later – shortly before the existing timber farmhouse was sold, disassembled and taken away – the couple were discussing design concepts for its replacement when their architect noticed their collection of flint. They decided then to create a contemporary farmhouse – a bridge between their past lives and their current, muddier, existence – from flint.

'The exterior completely exceeded our expectations,' says Phil. The minimal, hand-crafted flint facade follows the gentle slope of the hill and is interrupted by a single, vast, retractable window that opens up the entire front of the house. The design captivated the planners: 'We were surprised at how easily it sailed through planning,' says Michael. 'Their response was: "This is exactly how a modern house should fit into the landscape."'

The design deliberately demarcated work from pleasure. 'Working on a farm, you're covered in muck pretty much from the moment you walk out the door,' says Phil. 'It was lovely to be able to come home to a space that felt a bit special: it lifted the whole experience.'

On the lower floor an office, utility room and mud room ensured work remained separate from their personal space. Upstairs, the couple were able to reconnect with their previous selves in an open-plan living area defined by dark polished concrete floors, crisp, minimal lines and high ceilings. A playful concrete slope borders the edge of the layout, connecting the kitchen at one end of the slope to the master bedroom at the other.

The build came in on budget and was complete in just 12 months. Michael's advice to would-be self-builders is to give yourself enough time for the project and not to get carried away with initial ideas. 'Think about how the building is going to suit your everyday needs,' he says. 'A cantilever swimming pool would be great – but not if you don't like swimming!'

Unsurprisingly, the house attracted 'a constant stream of visitors'. It also became a backdrop for their new venture, the Two Cocks Brewery – a name they have previously described as 'memorable but not illegal'. Michael explains: 'The house had the same ethos as the brewery. Ecologically, it was about having a light touch and using the best locally sourced ingredients and materials.' Prospective stockists were welcomed into their home for tours and tastings.

Within the space of a few years, Phil and Michael had transformed their plot from a failing farm into 'an economic hub'. But as the farm prospered, Michael's mother's health was deteriorating. She moved into the

farm to live with them both shortly after the build was completed. They altered the function of the rooms on the ground floor to create a bedroom and living room for Michael's mother, who struggled with the number of stairs. 'We had designed the house for the stage of life we were at in that moment,' Michael reflects. 'What was an urbanised farm then suddenly had to become a care home ...'

The couple came to need something different. 'We felt we had done all we could to the farm – and we certainly left it in a better state than we found it,' Michael concludes. They sold the farm and brewing business in 2017 and moved to a Georgian manor house in Somerset. 'We don't do forever homes,' Phil explains. 'Neither of us really get that mentality.'

Michael traces this restlessness to their childhood experiences of home. Phil left Australia when he was young while Michael, whose mother was a German refugee, spent his childhood living abroad. 'There's nothing which firmly roots us to one place,' Phil explains. 'For a lot of people that would be a major negative, but for us, it's a huge positive. It gives us the freedom to go anywhere. We both love architecture and experiencing different types of houses. For us, the farm was just one of many. For us, home is not the building, it's memories you make while you're there.'

The Long View

At face value, exquisitely shaped architecture with excoriating white walls is not the most likely of bedfellows with the mud-drenched world that is farming. But then Michael and Phil are not your typical farmers. They wanted a weekend home as respite from their London jobs, a relaxing hideaway. Then they saw a Berkshire plot with 40 acres (16 hectares), a beaten-up wooden shack and an agricultural tie that stipulated that whoever lived there had to earn their living from the land.

Thus it was that Two Cocks Farm was born, an added-value modern agri-business with a micro-brewery and rare breeds. And, of course, a striking twenty-first century farmhouse to match.

That the worlds of their home and their farm could be separated so cleanly is thanks to architect Sara Gardhouse of Taate, who separated the living quarters from the world of 'agricultural deposits' both vertically (accommodation is all first floor) and sequentially (access to the house is via a 'mud lock', serviced with full drainage, shower heads and boot and clothing storage). It is an ingenious arrangement. It is an ingenious and remarkable home.

2013
—
Hangar
House
—
Strathaven

•	Episode aired	2013
•	Location	South Lanarkshire
•	Owner(s)	Colin and Marta
•	Architect(s)	Richard Murphy
•	Build cost	£500,000 (as of 2019)

It is impossible to think of the crinkly tin building put up by Colin and Marta without thinking of flying. Colin is a flying instructor, Marta defies gravity as a trapeze artist. Together they run an airfield in southern Scotland. For fun they will teach you how to ride a hovercraft.

So it is not surprising that in commissioning a home from the illustrious architect Richard Murphy (also a keen aviator) they both wanted to be up in the air. His response was an inverted house, with spare bedrooms and a garage on the ground floor and a first floor of all the usual living accommodation, like a giant floating apartment. Bedrooms offer pilot level views; upstairs in this airship is more first-class cabin.

Floating was perhaps one of the most important aspects of the brief. The two floors of the house appear disconnected and seem almost captured under a roof that has been tethered down. The agglomeration of shapes – boxes and curves connected with an exposed steel frame – suggests a futuristic airship ready to take flight.

The house serves as home for Colin and Marta but also as office and base for their business, running the busy adjacent airfield. In fact the house overlooks and sits right next to the airstrip, slightly distanced from, but in line with, the sequence of metal-clad hangars that house aircraft of all types. It is, as Marta describes it, 'the control tower of our airfield and the control tower of our lives'.

Gaining that control was, however, hard. It took most of a decade to finish the project. They used all their capital, sold a valuable painting and had to stop work after a hangar fire devastated the business. The eventual £100,000 insurance pay out

allowed them to complete the house: on a wing and a prayer, you might say.

Like an aluminium space frame (its nickname is Aluminia Meadownia), the building sparkles and reflects the sky; Colin and Marta agree it is a 'glamorous building ... like a sculpture'. However, the glint and polish come at a price: 'Metal cladding, you think low maintenance,' Colin admits, 'but, like a caravan, the north side gets a bit green over winter so in the spring I get out there with a sponge.' 'We get out there with a sponge,' Marta adds.

The choice of materials for this house, though seemingly wilful, was fundamentally practical. The airfield sits around 260m (850ft) above sea level and catches some vicious winds. The house needed to be as robust and as strong as the hangars. So Richard Murphy took industrial technology and cladding,

and designed the building with a thermally broken steel frame. Its visual cues come from the buildings on site, Richard's own love of flying and the capabilities of the materials. Plus inspiration from an unlikely source: the early steel-clad buildings of Glenn Murcutt, the Pritzker Prize-winning Australian architect. There is a family resemblance, though distant.

Marta and Colin's home is one of colourful, soaring living spaces articulated through a metal space frame, showcasing their joint love of art and landscape. It is a flying machine for living in, happily moored to the landscape but dreaming of reaching for the sky.

2014

—

Container House

—

County Derry

•	Episode aired	2014
•	Location	County Derry
•	Owner(s)	Patrick
•	Architect(s)	Patrick Bradley
•	Build cost	£135,000 (as of 2014)

Patrick was in his early thirties when he first appeared on *Grand Designs*. At the time, he was working as an architect from a shed on his parents' farm and becoming increasingly frustrated by the buildings going up around him. 'I just thought it would be quite nice to be able to practise what I preach,' he says. 'To build a contemporary house in the countryside and to do it on a small budget.' This simple aim set Patrick on a path that 'changed his life for the better'.

Patrick's parents entrusted him with an area on their farm that he describes as a 'rural Irish paradise'. Ancient trees, a crystalline stream and boulders robed in moss formed a landscape that had remained unchanged for centuries – which is why Patrick's plan to stack four shipping containers on top of one another was contentious. While the planners were eager to see his bold vision made real, Patrick's mother was concerned that his design would mar her favourite view on the farm.

The timescale for this project was 'manic'. The foundations were laid in May 2014; Patrick moved into his finished project in September that same year. 'I wanted to prove to myself as much as anybody else that I could do this on time and on budget,' Patrick says. 'I said to myself: "I've got one chance to do this: make this beautiful and make it right."'

It was a Herculean effort that, at times, required up to 30 tradespeople working together into the night. For Patrick, the most memorable day of the build began at dawn in his friend's building yard. 'That was a very, very nervous day for me,' he recalls. The team had assembled to mock-up the cruciform arrangement of the four reinforced shipping containers. 'In a matter of less than 20 minutes, the main frame of my house just went up,' Patrick says. The containers were then craned onto the back of lorries and driven to site, where the foundations had already been prepared. 'In the space of two hours, my house was just sitting there,' says Patrick. 'It was a really strange feeling that's hard to explain: it was just such an emotional, lovely day.'

Despite – or possibly because of – the physical demands of the job, Patrick forged life-long relationships while working on site. 'It's hard to describe how thankful I am for the connections and relationships it has brought me,' he says. 'It just gives me a smile every time I think back to the build. Such great times …'

Patrick designed and built his 115m^2 (1,238ft^2) home 10 years ago, but it was always intended to adapt to any changes in his personal life. 'A house shouldn't be designed for the here and now,' he says. 'It's about trying to make the building work for you for as long as possible.' He now lives at home with his wife and two young children. The only change they have made is the addition of a baby gate at the top and bottom of the stairs. 'It's minimal, it's simple, it's enjoyable,' he says of the space. 'This sounds crazy, but we hardly have any arguments, and I think that's because we're happy here: we've created something that everybody enjoys.'

His advice to anyone about to embark on their own self-build is to think about what they need, as opposed to what they want. Once the brief has been decided, preparation is key: 'A lot of people tend to start projects on a whim with no preparation. That's when they run into financial difficulties and stress – and that just shouldn't be the case. Think of all the risks, understand when they're going to arise and what you might have to do to overcome them. If you can put that effort into the preparation, then the actual build itself should be a breeze.'

The boldness of his vision and the tenacity with which he brought it to life put Patrick on the map professionally. Over the past decade, he has welcomed architecture enthusiasts from all over the world into his home. 'It's humbling to think that I've helped this idea of building from containers to evolve,' he says. 'That's what you have to do as an architect, to push boundaries. Ultimately, that's what good architecture is about – it's about changing people's lives for the better.'

The Long View

Since 2014, Patrick's home has remained among the strongest of favourites in the *Grand Designs* firmament, for so many reasons. The story of his growth from architect working on his family farm to running a successful practice is closely tied to the making of this building. The personal stories of his parents and sisters added warmth and a family context to our film. When we went back to see Patrick, we found him sharing his home with Victoria, the woman who became his wife and mother to his children.

The building also dealt with some urgent and important issues around sustainability. Over 60 per cent of the UK's waste comes from construction so Patrick's agenda was to use waste to build with, specifically four redundant shipping containers. He wanted minimum energy consumption in use, and he wanted to respect the biodiversity of where he was building – the house has no garden to speak of; it sits in farmland.

The unexpected result of this rigorous approach is a beautiful building which is innovative architecture, a result that has earned this house awards and international recognition.

2014
—
Engineered Timber House
—
North Cornwall

•	Episode aired	2014
•	Location	Cornwall
•	Owner(s)	Gregory and Rebecca
•	Arch. Designer	Gregory Kewish
•	Build cost	approx. £125,000 (as of 2015)

This is a fascinating and technical project, an experimental building that pushes at the limits of a building material – timber – and showcases the minds of two delightful, technical people: Gregory, who took his Master's in architecture in the States, and Rebecca, who is an accomplished lighting designer.

Essentially the house is simple and small, an overhanging timber first floor planted onto an ancient two room single-storey cottage. Each floor speaks a different language. The old cottage, built of local stone, was entirely traditional and vernacular, and Gregory and Rebecca worked hard to conserve that personality. Upstairs, however, the potential of wood was unleashed.

Gregory was intrigued by the process of cross-lamination, the creation of giant panels using planks of relatively poor-grade timber stacked and glued in alternating directions to produce a multi-layered giant version of plywood. The resulting cross-laminated timber (CLT) is super-strong and dimensionally stable, and has been in use for decades on the Continent as a structural component to replace steel and concrete.

But it has seen relatively little take-up in the UK. In 2013, when Gregory and Rebecca first explored CLT's potential, it was not well-known in Britain. Eleven years later, the architects Waugh Thistleton have constructed the first UK office block in Whitechapel using CLT. Meanwhile, in Norway, the world's first tower block to be built almost entirely of wood, Mjøstårnet, opened in 2019. It contains apartments, a hotel, offices and a restaurant, and showcases CLT and other glue-laminated technologies. It has since been rivalled by a taller timber tower, Ascent MKE in Milwaukee.

Glued wood now offers many of the engineering qualities traditionally brought by more carbon-intense traditional materials, while also sequestering carbon. You can make bridges with it (the French regularly do, spanning motorways using CLT), create huge domed spaces for sports arenas and build cantilevers and unsupported roof structures. Gregory did both of these, and went on to explore the use of CLT offcuts from his house to build furniture for their home. This house is an important showcase for the domestic use of this important building material of the future.

2015
—
Riverside Shed
—
South Downs

•	Episode aired	2015
•	Location	East Sussex
•	Owner(s)	Stephen and Anita
•	Architect(s)	Sandy Rendel
•	Build cost	£700,000 (as of 2015)

For Stephen, home is an elusive concept. 'I've lived a very nomadic life,' he explains. 'Even as a child, I don't think I stayed in one place for more than five years, so home is quite an alien concept for me.' The multi-award-winning contemporary house he built on the banks of the River Ouse in Lewes is no exception. 'I enjoyed the process so much that, even before it was finished, I was already thinking about doing it again ...'

Stephen sold the house in 2017, two years after completing the build. He has since undertaken two further major renovation projects. It may not embody the notion of 'home' for Stephen, but the house still holds sway: 'I really love the building,' he admits. 'Even now, I feel a real sense of accomplishment when I think of that project. I've never felt like that about any of the other buildings I've renovated.'

Situated on a narrow plot in beneath a chalk cliff face at the start of the town's main thoroughfare, the striking design is characterised by a delicate mesh of weathered steel and a fractured roofline, which cleverly echoes the rhythm of the existing streetscape. It was dubbed 'the gateway to Lewes' – a moniker that attracted the attention of planners and locals alike.

'Obviously, it's a house that polarised opinion,' says Stephen. 'But I've never been interested in doing anything that's bland in any aspect of my life – I want to provoke opinions.' When the building was complete and he and his then wife, Anita, had moved in with their baby daughter, they decided to invite everyone on the street around for a drink. 'We were expecting 10 or 12 people, but about 70 people turned up!' Stephen recalls. 'Some of these people had been airing their opinions about the house online, so I used the opportunity to politely confront them about it.'

In comparison to the drinks party, the build itself was relatively stress free. It was completed on budget within nine months, which Stephen attributes to the skill and professionalism of both his architect, Sandy Rendel, and his builder. A defective batch of raw steel resulted in a shipment of less-than-perfect

steel panels from Spain. The manufacturer gracefully accepted responsibility and replaced the panels, while the builder ensured the delay didn't have a knock-on effect on the already tight build schedule. Inside and out, the level of finish is exceptional.

Once our cameras had stopped rolling, all that remained to do was some gentle landscaping in the small areas of garden adjacent to the river: no other aspects of the design were altered. 'That's because a huge amount of thought went into it,' says Stephen. 'Sandy was responsible for the exteriors, but I sourced absolutely everything inside, all the way down to the light switches. I was thinking about this 24/7 before and during the build – nothing was left to chance.' In retrospect, Stephen thinks the open-plan kitchen, dining and living space would have benefited from 'some sort of division', but the constraints of the long, narrow site prevented that.

Interestingly, Stephen's next project – a four-storey Georgian town house in the centre of town – was much less easy to live in. 'Growing up, my mum was a single parent, and we never had any money, so I always had this ambition to live in a large house. But actually, my experience of that was quite disappointing,' he admits. 'We never even used the two formal living rooms on the ground floor. Although it was considerably smaller, the old house was a much better size to live in.'

The impact of the house on the town remains tangible. As a piece of contemporary architecture, Stephen is justly proud of its notoriety: 'Great cities or towns all have different buildings that begin to represent their own history. Lewes is a beautiful town with some amazing historical buildings – but there are also some pretty rotten modern buildings that have been built here in the last 30 years or so. This is the opposite of that: it's a great contemporary building that represents the best architecture of its time.'

The Long View

There are loaded words – words of approbation – that architects use to describe the best of their work. They include 'episodic', 'formal', 'narrative' and 'constraint' – and the word 'considered'. Considered is often reserved for the highest praise. It suggests that a consummately skilled architect has laboured night and day over every detail and reworked it to the point of elegant resolution; the very best outcome for that shadow gap in that building in that place.

In my mind I often revisit Stephen and Anita's house, designed by the eminent Sandy Rendel, remembering the staircase design, the theatrical dark hallway, the seemingly stitched industrial cladding, the splendid layout and the inventive first floor bedrooms that poke up into the roofscape where normally you'd expect to find just a dull sequence of cellular rectangles.

This is a beautifully resolved building, full of careful invention.

2015
—
Stilt House
—
East Sussex

•	Episode aired	2015
•	Location	East Sussex
•	Owner(s)	James
•	Architect(s)	Ben Hebblethwaite
•	Build cost	approx. £400,000 (as of 2015)

Riverbank people are such a rare, web-footed breed that they even have their own name: riparians. Like marshdwellers, another liminal subset, they slip between land and water, never fully occupying both and therefore never fully conforming to how the rest of us live nor to the dry laws that govern us. Theirs is an attitude chronicled in Graham Swift's fascinating novel, *Waterland*.

James is no exception. He wanted a house against the river, on stilts and built to live in – that would also be for boats. He wanted a workshop instead of another bedroom. He wanted a simple place to lock up and leave. He wanted a mast and a crows' nest to top his sedum roof: 'The white sofa brigade can go stuff themselves as far as I'm concerned.'

These design ideas ebbed and flowed like the tide during the design stages of the home and well after planning was granted, all of which gave Ben Hebblethwaite, James's nephew and his architect, the biggest of headaches. The conversations were vigorous: 'hot-headed' and 'reactionary,' as Ben puts it.

The building's success grew, not despite this constant questioning, but because of it. An early contractor went bust, taking £87,000 of James's money with him. And yet the design got better when the budget shrank. Ben interrogated the layouts and reworked the design to be as 'unhouselike' as possible, and the result was a series of simple shed shapes that seemed ready to shift and adapt to any purpose thrown at them. In other words, the house took on a true riparian identity, flexible and sometimes ambiguous in its response to its setting and its owner. James, in turn, grew delighted with it, becoming a slightly more comfortable landlubber.

2016
—
Tree House
—
Gloucestershire

•	Episode aired	2016
•	Location	Gloucestershire
•	Owner(s)	Jonathan and Noreen
•	Architect(s)	Millar Howard Workshop
•	Build cost	approx. £300,000 (as of 2023)

Jon's primary school playground overlooked an impenetrable patch of woodland in the centre of Dursley. Among the mature trees and locked behind closed gates was a climbing frame that remained frustratingly off limits. Several decades later, in 2012, Jon discovered that the same patch of woodland was up for sale. He approached the gates to take a closer look.

The climbing frame had disappeared, but the site still held promise: 'It was just before Christmas – the darkest part of the year,' Jon recalls. 'As I peered through the gates, I could see that the treetops were bathed in sunshine.' That golden scene set Jon and his wife, Noreen, on a lengthy journey that has transformed their lives and the future of this forgotten pocket of Dursley.

The plot was being sold without planning permission which, for Jon and Noreen, represented a huge financial risk. But the couple had found a local architect, Tomas Millar, who they were willing to put their faith in. 'We thought, if we ever get this house off the ground, he is the man for the job,' says Noreen. Tom's concept for the protected site became just that: a house that came off the ground.

To get through the protracted planning process, they had to submit plans for a building of outstanding architectural merit – 'something the planners want to see built.' They devised a structurally sophisticated design for three stacked, cantilevered boxes that rise up into the canopy without disturbing any of the trees.

The couple sold their high-maintenance Edwardian rectory to fund the project and moved into a cabin on site. They immediately encountered problems with the build and were living in cramped conditions for two years before the work even began. 'There were points at which we just thought, this is too hard,' admits Noreen. 'We had a dog, four cats and three rabbits that lived in a huge enclosure outside. At the time, we would joke that the rabbits had a larger space to live in than we did.'

For Noreen, anything that nudged the build closer to moving in was memorable. For Jon – a plumber by trade – it was the moment he dowsed for water on site and dug a borehole to reveal a sparkling pool of water at the bottom. (Aside from sewerage, their urban plot is entirely off grid.) In total, the couple spent three-and-a-half years living in the cabin before their home was ready to move into.

Despite the build overrunning, they managed to keep within budget. This was 'non-negotiable'. For them, the project represented an opportunity to redress their work–life balance. Jon's advice to anyone wishing to do the same is to 'be modest in your ambitions' and to 'always have a plan B for every design decision: a way of stepping back before you get to crunch point'.

Having lived up in the canopy for several years, the tribulations of the build have receded, the timber cladding has silvered and their home 'looks like it's always been here'. They've even recently converted the cabin into a weekend bolthole for additional income. Before the first pile went in, the couple planted 17 additional native and rare breed fruit trees as well as 16 rambling roses, which have wound their way around the perimeter of the woodland, filling the air with their scent come spring.

'Being just slightly raised up, our connection with wildlife really is that much more intense,' says Jon. 'From owls at night, to bats flying through the trees so close you can actually feel the draught from their wings on your face as they pass by – it's that intimacy with nature that I've really found very special.' For Noreen, the internal environment they've created is equally cherished: 'We've created a comfortable, welcoming space for our friends and families – a place that reflects our personalities and what's important to us.'

Their home is also a generous gesture that extends beyond their decking and out into the community. 'I hope it will help wildlife to thrive,' says Noreen, 'and I hope it will help Dursley to thrive, too.'

The Long View

I have nothing but admiration and support for Team Jon+Noreen. Noreen is a ceramicist with an acuity of perception and drive that is rare. Jon is a plumber and engineer who is also an artist and sustainability enthusiast with a particular interest in renewables. Together they are in effect a team of at least four people, with the energy and hope to match.

Their home is an exquisite blend of innovative construction, fly-by-wire engineering and super-lightweight groundworks. A school chemistry lab has been recycled and sports hall flooring reimagined, while agricultural metalwork and marble from a Rolls Royce showroom have been reused. It all floats above a woodland floor where the couple grow food and tend to their trees with innovative and biodynamic forestry techniques.

There is not a single thing to dislike in this home and so much that is exemplary.

2016
—
Shadow Barn
—
Horsham

•	Episode aired	2016
•	Location	West Sussex
•	Owner(s)	Matt and Sophie
•	Architect(s)	MATT Architecture
•	Build cost	£840,000 (as of 2016)

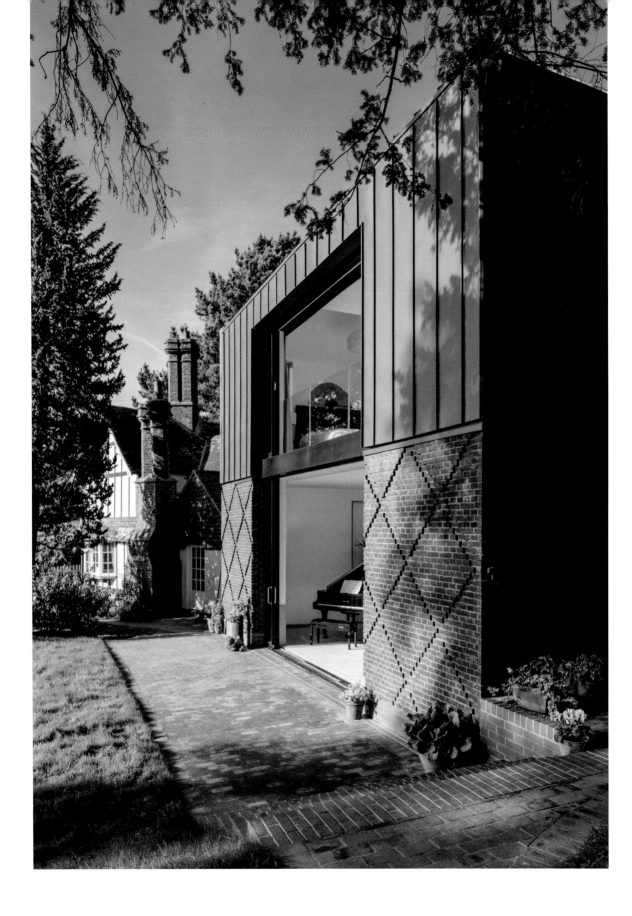

Ten years ago Matt and Sophie were renting a home in Sussex for their family while rebuilding another in London where they jointly run Matt's practice. Then they spotted a small and sweet gatekeeper's lodge for sale on a country estate near their rental. It was too small to live in, so Matt immediately produced plans to enlarge it with an extension that grew in scale to become a huge black barn. They bought the place, decisions changed and they landed on a plan to live temporarily in the lodge, finish the London house and rent it out before being able, finally, to live in the barn/lodge.

This is one version of events. There are almost certainly several others.

One of which is a children's story that has at its core an imaginative delight in play and fun. Matt is not alone as an architect who enjoys freeing himself in his work – Jean Nouvel said that he likes to play with architecture; it's his favourite game – and so, in that spirit, the big black barn grew alongside the gingerbread gatekeeper's lodge. As it grew, the barn became not a dreadful dark place, but instead a large friendly shadow behind the lodge.

Outside, it grew a crust of black patterned brick and wore a coat of long metal, as if Issey Miyake had designed a suit of armour for it.

It looked serious and powerful and yet it had a kind heart. It spoke gently to the little gingerbread house that sat in its shadow – and the gingerbread house smiled and knew secretly that one day soon it too would be painted and looked after.

Meanwhile the barn's heart and soul were slowly brightening and evolving into a house of fun, of 'white clean, usable space,' as Matt likes to call it, full of hidden staircases, secret panels, Scooby-doo revolving doors and playful details everywhere. The house would have been tickled pink if it weren't already white.

Hindu spiritual leader Chinmayananda Saraswati once called children the 'architects of the future world'. Architects meanwhile are busy building the world's tomorrows for our children. In Matt and Sophie's barn those tomorrows are filled with play.

2017
—
Extruded Barn
—
County Down

•	Episode aired	2017
•	Location	County Down
•	Owner(s)	Micah and Elaine
•	Architect(s)	Micah Jones
•	Build cost	£245,000 (as of 2017)

The construction of Micah and Elaine's family home is a tale of extraordinary expediency and slow, determined progress. It began in 2014, when the couple first found a dilapidated stone barn in rural County Down. They sold their terraced house in Belfast, but it took a further eighteen months for the purchase of the plot to go through.

During that time Micah, an architect, and his wife, Elaine, were able to 'tweak and fiddle' with the design for the barn: a robust, 240m² (2,580ft²) space with four bedrooms on the ground floor, and a bright, open-plan living space on the first floor with far-reaching views of the Mourne Mountains.

The family – which then included two young boys and a third child on the way – moved into a cramped caravan on site as work began in April 2016. The original stone structure was quickly demolished, and the pressure was immediately on to get out of the ground. 'Normally, builders would take two or three months to get to first floor level,' Micah explains. 'We had three weeks to get the whole ground floor built before the cross-laminated timber for the first floor arrived.'

The arrival of the timber frame was another moment of 'true jeopardy'. Torrential rain had turned their long, narrow country lane into a perilous track which no lorry driver had risked before the arrival of Gerhardt from Austria. He remained 'completely unfazed,' despite his vehicle needing a final nudge from the digger.

With a 'shoestring budget' of £245,000, the rapid pace of the build consumed funds quickly.

In February 2017 – just 10 months after the build began – they moved into a building that was far from finished. Most of the internal fit out was left for Micah to complete in the evenings and weekends. 'It was down to me to crack on with it,' he says.

His approach was mindful and methodical: 'When you're doing it on your own, you don't see a lot of progress, so you have to get your mind in the right place, otherwise it can get very overwhelming,' he says. 'I just plodded on, knowing that if I managed to lay just 1m² (11ft²) of stonework, then I was one step further forward.' Elaine, meanwhile, was solely responsible for meeting the day-to-day needs of their family. 'Our approach was very much divide and conquer,' says Micah.

With the budget spent, the fit out was completed with recycled remnants. The staircase, kitchen island and even the multi-coloured tiled wall were all constructed from offcuts of timber. 'Everywhere we could, we were trying to find creative ways of making something quite ordinary into something special,' Micah says.

It took the family some months to expand into the new space and for Micah, the adjustment was emotional as well as spatial. 'I knew the building almost too well,' he says. 'For the first two or three years, all I could see were problems or jobs that hadn't quite been sorted. But I suppose, like any relationship, the longer you're together, the more accepting you become. There comes a point when you have to stop putting quite so much energy in and just live.'

The family have lived in their barn for seven years now. Externally, moss and ivy have softened the edges of the stonework which now 'looks like it's been there for 20 years'. The trees they planted have started to mature and the construction of a new garage has created an enclosed courtyard, which was part of the original design. They have added solar panels to the roof and the caravan they lived in for the duration of the build is now Micah's own studio.

Internally, there's just one thing left on the agenda. 'When the kids were small, there wasn't any need for internal doors because we were constantly in the same space, and they enjoyed tearing up and down on their tricycles,' says Micah. 'As the kids have got older, there is more of a need for that separation ...'

Their warm, straightforward house is, according to Micah, a reflection of their approach to life: 'It's not a pit that we've had to throw all our money into,' he says. 'There is scope to do other things and to have more to life than just a house.' Like the campervan they have parked in their new garage. 'We go away a lot,' says Micah. 'But everyone always loves coming home. The house has given us a huge amount of freedom and that freedom is part of what makes it home.'

The Long View

Micah is an architect who has grown up in a family of artists and of sheds. During filming I think I counted 19 current sheds in his life, from tumbledown garages to summer houses and brick outhouse workshops, as well as the caravan he adapted for family living and which now houses his practice. Micah knows a thing or two about shed life.

Elaine is a force of nature, a galvanising element in Micah's world to provide shape and purpose. I hope they both recognise these characterisations. Together they are a formidable couple who have become experts in the 'Just Enough' school of life. They know how to deliver Just Enough architecture (with maybe a little extra) with Just Enough decoration and delight, for Just Enough money.

Of course, in recognising and delivering just enough, every time, they have built a home and a private world of infinite richness, fun and quality. That is the paradoxical nature of Just Enough theory.

2017

—

Earth-sheltered House

—

Peak District

•	Episode aired	2017
•	Location	Derbyshire
•	Owner(s)	Fred and Saffron
•	Architect(s)	Client + Akiva Lawson
•	Build cost	approx. £800,000 (as of 2017)

If architecture should reflect people and place (which it very much should) then Fred and Saffron's home deserves to be recognised as a model project. Fred grew up in the village where they built (he took a hit on the price when selling his previous home just to enshrine affordability in this part of the Peak District, popular with incomers and second home owners); as a professional ecologist he also wanted an entirely nature-friendly zero carbon home.

They were both sensitive to the visual impact of what they were building, but getting planning permission (in a national park) still took seven years. They won because the planners conceded the building would do no harm and would enhance the setting. Saffron delivered, working alongside a local design-and-build firm to construct a house built into the steep slope of a valley, almost entirely hidden and capped with a beautifully wrought timber and stone studio building, a modest, seemingly isolated contribution to the architecture of the historic village and the only part of their house visible from the street.

Their home was built with local labour, local help and local stone. Family pitched in and the resulting building is a marvel of near-vertical slope construction filled with pipework cables and ducting – all on proud and polished display – that speak of the building's determination to mine heat from the rock and the sun and to use it, alongside fresh air and wondrous views, to look after its human contents.

The late-nineteenth century designer and campaigner, William Morris, said: 'Have nothing in your houses that you do not know to be useful or believe to be beautiful.' Fred and Saffron have crafted a building with a taut and rigorous ecological aesthetic, deriving its visual identity from a blend of craftsmanship and function, finding beauty in the deep green performance of insulated shutters, exquisite joinery and attentively pointed blockwork. It is a joy to behold and to live in, and an example of how we can look after our planet by allowing its rocky structure to look after us.

2018
—
Concrete House
—
Lewes

•	Episode aired	2018
•	Location	East Sussex
•	Owner(s)	Adrian and Megan
•	Architect(s)	Graeme Laughlan of Raw Architecture Workshop
•	Build cost	approx. £500,000 (as of 2020)

Thinking back to the standout moments of their pioneering self-build project, Adrian and Megan are reminded of an evening spent working deep down in the footings of what is now their sunken lounge. 'We were losing the light, so we were down in the mud using our phone torches, arguing with each other,' Megan recalls. 'It was a crappy time,' adds Adrian. 'There was just mud everywhere and you look around thinking, this build will literally never happen.'

Thankfully, they were able to see the funny side: 'We suddenly thought what if somebody walking past could hear us arguing in the bottom of a glowing hole and we just burst out laughing,' says Megan. 'Forget death or divorce,' says Adrian. 'Building your own house is as stressful as it gets. If you're in a rocky relationship, my advice would be just do not do it!'

Their indomitable spirit and sense of humour drove this determinedly different project – an uncompromising, multi-level family home constructed entirely of concrete. Their design was inspired by a stay in a concrete villa in Mexico and a long-held love of Brutalist architecture. 'It might sound slightly odd,' says Adrian, 'but I wanted the space to be less about what it looked like and more about what it sounded and felt like: there had to be a tactility and calmness to it – both qualities you get from concrete.'

Their sensory space took shape over four years, which Adrian describes as a creative and collaborative process between themselves, the architect, Graeme Laughlan, and their local planning officer. The build itself took 18 months, during which time the couple and their three children moved out of their existing bungalow and into an on-site caravan. 'We survived six months in there before moving to a rental nearby,' says Megan.

The couple collaborated with a multi-national cement manufacturer at the forefront of emerging manufacturing techniques. Their heavily insulated home was designed without the need for reinforcing bars. Instead, the structural elements of the building were to be made from a fibre-reinforced, self-compacting concrete. Even the reusable formwork (the hollow moulds the concrete is poured into) were to be made from recycled plastics. 'Our home is now used globally as a case study for a sustainable concrete build,' Adrian explains.

Despite the inherent pressures and unknowns of working with a highly experimental product, both Adrian and Megan relished the anticipatory process of removing the formwork. 'I remember walking around the site one spring evening with the walls rising up from the slab and just seeing the space emerge,' says Megan. Adrian was similarly struck by the immediacy of the raw material: 'You could put your hand on the wall and know that this is how it would look and feel. It was an incredible feeling.'

With the budget spent, the interiors remained unfinished when they moved in. 'We practically

camped inside for the first year,' says Megan. Their kitchen was cobbled together from pieces of ply, a salvaged sink and the old site fridge. 'Trying to make any of those final decisions in the midst of the build was beyond us,' Megan admits. 'I've never really understood why people spend all their money on kitchens and cushions before moving in,' Adrian adds. 'It's really only living in the space that can inform the design direction.'

After five years, they have settled into the space, which now functions as a shoot and film location. The external concrete has faded to pale grey. Contrary to the common misconception that concrete 'sits heavy on the ground', Adrian describes how the weathered and windowless front facade – which is hunkered into the ground at the same level as the original bungalow – almost fades into the sky.

Locally, their home continues to confound passers-by, which enthrals Adrian: 'People aren't sure if the building is a wartime bunker or a commercial premises that we've adapted,' he says. 'I love that! I find it fascinating that our home invokes such a strong reaction. The last thing we want is for anyone to tell us that they think our home is nice: I'd rather someone said they either hate it or love it, and that is something this house seems able to do. To this day, that continues to give me great joy.'

The Long View

Obsession is a strong word but at the margins of the self-build community it is bandied about frequently. Given how hard it is to build anything at all to any reasonable standard, obsession is a necessary quality when trying to do anything out of the ordinary. Adrian and Megan's home employed a relatively new concrete technology where small inch-long steel 'staples' or fibres fill the concrete mix to replace the enormous quantity of reinforcing bars normally used.

So, to avoid the slumping of the steel fibres in a pour, the gunking up of the concrete pump by said fibres, cracking, failure, concrete blowouts and structural defects, the only weapons they had were vigilant obsession and obsessive vigilance.

This project was a triumph of the improbable: the pursuit of a low energy, highly insulated concrete home, made doubly difficult by the methodology for the concrete itself. Enough to run you ragged. Unless you're an obsessive.

2018
—
Expedient House
—
Leominster

•	Episode aired	2018
•	Location	Herefordshire
•	Owner(s)	Steph and Alex
•	Architect(s)	Jessica Barker of Stolon Studio
•	Build cost	£270,000 (as of 2018)

There are multiple pitfalls for the self-builder, traps into which the many flaws in human nature lead us. One such pitfall is called Hubris, another Vanity, a third Seduction.

Steph avoided the first and second; her ambitions were too noble to begin with. She had spent 20 years dreaming of owning the farmland that her grandfather had sold, until the day she remortgaged the home she and her husband Alex owned and was able, remarkably, to buy 27 acres (11 hectares) of the land back.

This felt like redemption. Steph had always kept animals and this was going to be proper farming, with a home built on the land where she played as a child.

It was going to be a beautiful cantilevered building and the design was seductive. It was expensive, too, costed at £500,000, twice what she and Alex could afford.

Anyone else might have been snared by the Seduction, then might have begged, borrowed and wrangled their way to a shoddily built version of what they had hoped for: a compromise cantilever or a hashed home. Steph, however, sidestepped a fourth pitfall, Arrogance, and pragmatically asked for help from her childhood friend Jessica Barker, who just happened to be an award-winning architect. Jessica designed them a simple, unfussy barn of a building with more than its share of delight, beauty and clever practicality.

This was a rare tale, the story of a successful building and a successful outcome, of a process entirely free of indulgence and giddiness but instead rooted in the practical, careful everyday decision-making that farmers are famous for. So often we borrow too much and splash the cash, succumbing to all kinds of weaknesses and distractions. It usually makes for a compromised life and a fair few regrets. Steph and Alex were brave enough to change their direction, recalibrate and build something that was just enough.

2019
—
Watershed
—
Hull

•	Episode aired	2019	
•	Location	East Riding of Yorkshire	
•	Owner(s)	Richard and Felicia	
•	Arch. Consultant	Sense of Space Architects	
•	Build cost	approx. £230,000 (predicted)	

This singular home is nestled into the site of a former underground reservoir on the outskirts of a village in the East Riding of Yorkshire. The cavernous concrete structure was built in the late 1950s to hold 2.5 million litres (more than 550 thousand gallons) of water. Dark, dank and disused, there are few who could have imagined the possibility of forming a home in this vast, inhospitable bunker. Richard, an engineering consultant, is an exception: 'An engineering brain has the capacity – far more than anyone else – to form a relationship with an inanimate object,' he argues.

That relationship began on the very first site visit. Richard recalls the hair-raising experience: 'It was very, very spooky. There was about a foot of water in the cave-like structure, and it was drenched in condensation with drips echoing off into the distance. Staring down into the hole, a piece of wall came away and struck me on the back of my neck. I have a very rational brain, but that did give me a strange, shivery moment. It was as if the building was reaching out to me.' Richard felt compelled to decide whether the building was friend or foe.

'I decided it was a friend, and really, it's been friendly to me ever since.'

The portentous plot was bought from Yorkshire Water in 2010. Demolition work began apace four years later. That same year, Richard was diagnosed with prostate cancer. He underwent an operation and subsequently suffered blood poisoning, which put the entire project on hold for seven months. As part of his lengthy recovery process, Richard enrolled on a mindfulness course which he describes as 'a bit of an eye opener – this idea of being in the moment ...'

It's an approach that has affected what is a very personal, ongoing journey for Richard, who is still 'about £60,000 and six months of uninterrupted work' away from completing the build. 'I can't see what's wrong with being on the journey,' he says. 'When you live in an unfinished space, what you're actually doing is surrounding yourself with very positive potential.'

The design has been dictated by the budget and the constraints of the existing, earth-sheltered site. 'It doesn't follow anything else,' Richard explains. 'In that respect, I think it's timeless.' By integrating the concrete walls and floor of the original structure into the design, Richard has calculated that it would have cost £250,000 to build a similar structure, consuming 9 million litres (nearly 2.5 million gallons) of water and 600 tonnes of CO_2 in the process.

The unfinished nature of the build – though unfathomable for many – plays into the overarching concept for the site. 'The whole thing is designed to have versatility in use,' he explains. For example, the site's original valve tower was initially conceived as an office space. Before it eventually settles into its intended use, it currently functions as a welding shop. 'It's the only place in the whole building with a concrete floor,' Richard explains. He recently used the tower to craft a gate that hangs across the main entrance to the courtyard; it is a reformed web of steel bars salvaged from the roof of the reservoir.

The mutability of the interiors is facilitated by the fine steel frame Richard designed and procured while in recovery. 'I got quite emotional when the steel frame arrived,' he admits. 'When that went up, it gave us a pencil outline: you could actually see and feel the scale of the final building.' The structure of the frame permits complete freedom of use: with no supporting

walls the space remains truly versatile. 'Anyone coming to this building in future will be able to bring their own individuality to it,' says Richard.

Not that that will be happening any time soon. Eventually, Richard imagines he might divide the space into three dwellings, retaining his own separate wing. 'It's been an incredibly fulfilling, once-in-a-lifetime process that hasn't been disappointing at all,' he reflects.

Externally, the larch cladding has silvered and settled into the site. The surrounding concrete walls could do with resealing, and there are plans in place for some architectural planting in the courtyard, though Richard freely admits gardening is not his forte. There is one plant that he is keen to nurture, though: a small sprig of ivy that has self-seeded at the foot of the external concrete wall. 'It's only about 6in (15cm) above the ground, but I've grown very fond of it,' he admits. 'I want to see what happens to it. In some ways, I think I'm like that little sprig of ivy climbing up the wall: the longer I'm here, the more the building becomes part of me.'

The Long View

The Watershed is, as you'd expect from a creative engineer, maverick. Even its premise and its site are unusual. And in this Richard exemplifies the kind of self-builder we need: individuals who are prepared to sacrifice so much that is conventionally safe and easy for an idea that reshapes them as individuals and moves them from the mainstream to the margins. Buildings are not us, but they sometimes come to help define who we are more clearly. Among the ancient concrete, super-elegant steel and repurposed rubble, Richard repurposed himself.

And I will always be grateful for our conversations in which, among many other things, Richard confirmed for me an ancient truth that is held in high regard in Japanese Shintoism: that as we build and use engineered structures, machines and houses, they grow souls.

2019
—
Lighthouse
—
North Devon

•	Episode aired	2019
•	Location	Devon
•	Owner(s)	Edward and Hazel
•	Architect(s)	Alan Phillips
•	Build cost	approx. £6 million (as of 2022)

What is it that pushes humans to the brink? Is it hope that leads us to the edge of a cliff and then cheerfully pushes us off? Is it over confident self-belief and vanity that cloud our judgement? Or the hubris of needing to memorialise ourselves in something that might outlast us?

These and many other reasons, perhaps. Yet without these failings no great buildings will have ever been constructed. Risk and construction go hand in hand and the tension of building something original and sometimes unproven is compelling; it leads us to those unexplored areas of human endurance and brilliance – that show themselves when we suffer hardship and extreme stress – and shows us what we are capable of.

Edward and Hazel found themselves being led by their project into these uncharted waters. They demolished their tired clifftop house in North Devon to build a glamorous headland home replete with infinity pool, annexe and its own lighthouse. It turned out to be a painful story of strife, difficult construction, financial turmoil, and ultimately overreaching ambition. It was sad and difficult to witness, and the first screened episode struck a chord with viewers who understood and sympathised with Edward, as he shouldered the project alone and inched it forwards to an uncertain future.

Difficult too for the architect, Alan Phillips, who supported Edward throughout. The dedication paid off: when we revisited in 2022, 10 years after work had begun, the house was all but complete. Against overwhelming odds Edward had pushed and achieved the near impossible; he had straddled the cliff edge and not succumbed. He had built his house. 'The disaster for me would have been not to finish this ... I've lost weight but I haven't lost my mind.' Edward's honesty and openness, as ever, are disarming.

Nor had he entirely lost control of the project, despite vast costs, spending 'probably £200,000 on refurbishing everything' that had been damaged over a decade by salt water spray, and a total of between £5.5 to £6 million, all with the help of a property development lender. Needless to say, the debt incurred means that Edward cannot afford to live in the house which its new owners will no doubt come to love as much as he does.

Now back from the brink, the house is a marvel, offering a constant horizon view. Alan's design centres on the lighthouse, placed first and foremost on the promontory to survey the ocean, the rocks below and the swirling surf. Edward delights in this part of the house, topped by the storm room, to his core: 'Inside is like outside ... the world of the Atlantic changing in front of you.' It is, as he says, his 'little boy's dream space. A bubble in the middle of the North Atlantic. Epic'.

In 2019 I described this project as a cautionary tale of over-reaching ambition. Three years later Edward, Alan and their team had reversed the lighthouse's fortunes and rewritten its story as one of redemption, of closure and of the triumph of positive human energy.

2021
—
Pond House
—
Chichester

•	Episode aired	2021
•	Location	West Sussex
•	Owner(s)	Daniel and Nina
•	Arch. Designer	Daniel Rowland of Studio Fuse
•	Build cost	£750,000 (as of 2024)

Daniel didn't sleep the night before we arrived for the final day of filming. 'That partly explains why I looked so haggard,' he recalls. Daniel had worked doggedly throughout the night to ensure the house was ready for the final reveal. Walking downstairs in a fresh outfit before the cameras started rolling was momentous for him: 'It was the first time I had seen the house anything like finished,' he says. 'The machinery, scaffolding towers and paint cans had all been cleared away. For the first time, I could see clear surfaces and I thought: "We might have actually pulled this off!"'

In 2016, Daniel and his wife Nina set out to find a new home for their young family to grow up in. For Daniel, an architectural designer, that meant creating an environment inseparable from its surroundings. The plot they purchased was on the edge of a Site of Special Scientific Interest (SSSI) and within an Area of Outstanding Natural Beauty (AONB) in West Sussex. Undeterred by the stagnant pond in the garden, they moved into the dilapidated 1930s house and set to work reimagining the water-logged site.

Architecturally, their ambition was to design a home with a natural palette of materials: flint, silvered Siberian larch cladding and slate. 'The front elevation is deliberately more modest,' explains Daniel. 'It gets a bit more exciting at the back …' At the rear of the property, they created a carefully calibrated natural swimming pond that wraps around the building, beckoning them in for a dip on a near daily basis.

'We can't believe quite how much it enriches our lives every single day,' explains Daniel. 'The mantra that I had in my head from the beginning was to create a happy, healthy living environment for the family – a place for them to explore and have adventures and thrive as individuals and with friends. To have this lovely, natural environment as a backdrop to our lives is certainly life enhancing.'

Three years since the build, the pristine pond is teeming with wildlife: newts, kingfishers, herons, grass snakes and deer are all part of the picture here. The pond has also become a fulcrum for family, friends and the wider community, be it a class of primary school kids with pond-dipping equipment and inflatable unicorns or a cold water immersion experience for like-minded adults.

Inside, the generosity of space encourages spontaneous daily rituals. 'The girls use the space in the kitchen for dancing and cartwheels,' says Daniel. 'Sometimes in the morning, we'll do a little yoga routine together, then go for a dip in the pond before having breakfast and getting to school. It is a big house, but it's not in any way grandiose,' he continues. 'There's a joyous freedom in the size of it that means we're able to inhabit it in a vibrant and interesting way.'

Renewable energy systems – including a ground source heat pump, photovoltaic panels, solar energy

battery storage and highly insulated panels – have ensured their energy consumption remains minimal. 'We never turn the heating on on the top two floors,' says Daniel.

Over the past three years, Daniel has been 'chipping away' at unfinished projects. Inside, he has created a first floor studio and meeting place for their expanding biophilic architectural practice, Studio Fuse, which aims to integrate design with nature. Outside, he has recently converted a floating cabin into a sauna which – along with the woodfired hot tub – has enabled them to offer therapeutic day retreats that combine their passion for yoga and cold water immersion.

For Nina, the experience has completely altered her notion of home. In contrast to the worn-out house they lived in for six years before and during the build, their house represents a 'therapeutic sanctuary': a space that oscillates between providing an invigorating hub for like-minded folk (they recently hosted a birthday party for a hundred guests); and a soothing, restorative haven when needed (a month before her death, Nina's mother was here, floating in the pond with the dragonflies). 'Really, this home can be anything and everything you need it to be,' she says.

The Long View

The hook for this project that snagged everyone on the *Grand Designs* production team was not Dan's architecture – which, it turned out, was very good, joyful and mature. It wasn't the amenity value of the natural swimming pond or the arrangement of the kitchen across a little brook right up against the water. It was the stated claim that Dan and Nina were going to take a site with an existing house on it and improve the biodiversity on it – to the point where it would be more ecologically rich than any of the farmland around it.

The subsequent story of biodiversity net gain – a hugely important issue in architecture, planning and landscape management – was offset by a personal story of loss with the passing of Dan's father. In the end the rehabilitation of their site into a wildlife paradise became all the more emotionally powerful and redemptive.

2021

—

Self-heating House

—

Bletchley

	Episode aired	2021
•	Location	Buckinghamshire
•	Owner(s)	Andrew and Margretta
•	Architect(s)	Eco Design Consultants
•	Build cost	£310,000 (as of 2020)

The numbers are more or less established: the built environment is responsible for around 40 per cent of all greenhouse gas (GHG) emissions and that figure includes the carbon cost of first, mining, processing and constructing our made world (about 10 per cent of all GHG) plus second, the cost of powering, heating and cooling it (a little under 30 per cent).

That last figure is sobering. A whopping third of all greenhouse gas emissions come from keeping us comfortable inside buildings: not too hot, not too cold, but just right. This is our Goldilocks world.

So any building that can reduce energy in use needs to be noticed, and any building that can do so in a radical new way needs to be championed. Andrew has a PhD in Low Energy Systems and the home that he built for himself, his wife Margretta and his family, makes an important contribution to the debate.

Most earth-sheltered buildings use soil as a thermal stabiliser, taking advantage of the capacity of the ground to retain solar heat – below about 1.5m (5ft) the soil temperature is much more stable and less prone to fluctuation than at the surface. Andrew wanted to strip his buried concrete home

of its insulation and instead insulate the earth above its structure so that he could use that earth as a thermal battery, a store into which he could pump summer heat for use in winter.

As I ascertained from Andrew two years later, it's working. In summer, a pump circulates a coolant liquid under the concrete floor in the places where the sunshine lands (the house has no solar shading and even on an unusually warm 42°C (107°F) summer's day remains very cool). The heat is deposited straight into the earth battery. In winter it is recirculated back out into the structure, delivering temperatures well above 16°C (61°F). Andrew hopes that in time this home may require no additional heating or cooling at all.

We count ourselves lucky to be invited to film projects like this – and chronicle our collective journey on the road to zero carbon.

2021
—
Triangle House
—
Billingshurst

•	Episode aired	2021
•	Location	West Sussex
•	Owner(s)	Olaf and Fritha
•	Design	Olaf
•	Build cost	£280,000 (as of 2023)

Olaf's self-build in West Sussex was the first time he had 'gone the whole hog' – buying, designing, procuring, managing and building his own home. It was also the first time he and his partner, Fritha, had taken out a mortgage. The couple had met five years previously and were undergoing IVF treatment at the same time as the build. Technically, financially and emotionally, this complicated plot presented a series of unknowns.

Groundworks began in 2020 and quickly unearthed one major problem. Already constricted by a railway, a busy road and a sewer, the discovery of a second, unknown trunk sewer on site made an unforeseen dent in their self-build mortgage. Further excavation of the site revealed that the land wasn't solid. They needed to remove a tonne of earth from each square metre (11ft^2) of the plot before the foundations could be laid.

Undeterred, Olaf, who designs and builds bespoke interiors for a living, picked up a cereal box and made a model. Spurred on by Fritha's faith in his creative and technical abilities, he designed an 'enforced oddity' – a soaring, triangular structure that resolved the difficult constraints of the plot. 'I told Olaf to think of this as his PhD,' says Fritha. 'We both knew that he had to build this house.'

Laying the foundations was 'such a great feeling' that the couple buried a bottle of champagne in the footings to mark the occasion. Another memorable, life-changing moment was captured by us on film when Fritha took a pregnancy test in the on-site Portaloo. 'That actually happened,' says Olaf. Their daughter, Lagertha, was due in March, which added to the momentum of the build.

As the global pandemic pushed up the cost of building materials, they rushed to order windows, timber and insulation. With the additional groundworks they had already completed, their original self-build mortgage of £194,000 didn't last long. Eventually, they managed to increase their loan to £246,000 – which Olaf describes as 'the worst process of the entire build.' A further £30,000 loan from family members saw them through to completion.

Olaf didn't deviate from his early vision for their home: 'It was just a case of bringing it to fruition,' he says. They moved into their three bedroom,

123m² (1,324ft²) home in summer 2021: 'When the filming ended, it did leave a bit of a hole in our lives,' says Olaf. They needed to reset, so they went away on holiday and returned rejuvenated. 'We finished the kitchen and filled it with our stuff – now it really is a home.'

Initially, their 'stuff' threatened to overwhelm the space. 'Neither one of us has ever really had a place to call home,' Olaf explains. 'When all our stuff eventually made its way here, we realised we had double of everything.' Though they have utilised every inch of storage space, the house wasn't designed to contain their combined possessions. 'We're getting much braver at getting rid of stuff,' says Fritha. 'We know now that we actually don't need to hold on to so much.'

Outside on the driveway, the double decker bus Olaf manoeuvred into position during the build has had an extensive refit and now houses his 'small but functional' carpentry workshop and office space. He has even managed to install a woodburning stove and boiler that blows hot air through the existing heating system. Solar panels on the roof will generate an additional 60 per cent of energy.

Despite the temptation to furnish each bedroom with bespoke joinery, the couple have made the decision to keep the bedrooms as flexible as possible. As foster carers, this enables them to provide respite care for children in need of their own safe and welcoming space. 'When kids come to stay with us, they are really excited by the creativity and colour,' explains Olaf. 'They love the glass portal in the kitchen ceiling that gives a view right through to the top of the house, or they jump on miniature bikes and cars and pedal through the house and out across the drive. It's like a playground,' he says. 'They love it here.'

The village loves it, too. 'It has become a bit of a landmark,' says Olaf. When they opened their doors to the public during the local Heritage Weekend, they welcomed a continuous flow of around three hundred visitors each day. 'Everyone was so lovely. The reception of this house and the architecture has just been extraordinary.'

The Long View

Inevitably, the projects that viewers remember are those that overrun and overspend, usually spectacularly. These are uncontrollable and vainglorious schemes which cannot be shaken from the mind; inevitably they are dragged up and skewered by journalists and commentators wanting to hang our two-hundred-odd projects on a sharp and easy hook.

The truth, however, is that many self-builders construct modest and affordable homes. Olaf and Fritha's home was just such a fabulous example: complex and tightly formed, a small and lovingly made home as a vessel for that love to flourish within their growing family. And it represented the true jeopardy of building: of being able to conjure masterful spatial experiences, economy, enjoyment and well-made details on a meagre budget. The secret weapon in this was Olaf, a craftsman of phenomenal powers who was capable of transforming concrete blocks and rubbish firewood into beauty and delight.

2021
—
Gardener's Bothy
—
Kinross

•	Episode aired	2021
•	Location	Perth and Kinross
•	Owner(s)	Iain and Jenny
•	Architect(s)	Iain Shillady of Staran Architects
•	Build cost	£400,000 (as of 2021)

Although British housing is some of the smallest and meanest in Europe, when given the chance we will max out. I call it 'McMansion's Law', which dictates that any self-built home must creep as close as it possibly can to the plot's boundary – regardless of how many windows will face a neighbour's brick wall. Moreover, the distance to the boundary is in inverse proportion to the taste and discretion of the owner.

Iain and Jenny's dilemma was entirely different. Their site was generous and included a historic garden, bounded by a tall stone wall which divided their plot into two. Iain, an architect, is well-versed in dealing with historic buildings in Edinburgh and his design doesn't just approach this central boundary wall but cling to it. On the north side they took an existing gardener's workshop and converted it to bedrooms, gently retrofitting it with insulation to bring it up to habitable standards. On the south side they added a lower single-storey extension, a modern black timber box. All very discreet.

The tabloid newspapers took them to task for punching through the wall to make a doorway to connect the two halves; for obtaining planning permission on a Grade II listed site; for daring to think boldly. All of which ignored the problems that existed across the wider site which had previously been subdivided and rearranged. Jenny and Iain's subtle reworking, which combines revitalisation of the gardens, restoration of a wreck and a stealthy new build, has instead energised the place. Such is the power of investment, both in terms of money and human energy.

And their thoughtful and considered building demonstrates something else: what I call 'the theory of Just Enough' (see page 185). This is the opposite of McMansion's Law. It prescribes that we should all of us question how much stuff, space, storage and complication we need in our lives. It applies to buildings, cars, spoons and cities. Iain and Jenny have Just Enough architecture here. Nothing seems indulgent (other than the enormous skylight over the flat-roofed kitchen, invisible from all around and so necessary at this latitude for winter light). There is just enough conservation and repair work and low carbon conversion, and just enough contemporary space.

From this comes the architecture of modesty.

2022
—
Spacesaver
—
Sydenham Hill

•	Episode aired	2022
•	Location	South East London
•	Owner(s)	Corinne
•	Architect(s)	Simon Skeffington of Architecturall
•	Build cost	£678,000 (as of 2022)

Corinne was sitting in her home office overlooking the triangular plot at the side of her Sixties terrace in Sydenham Hill, South East London. 'I thought to myself: "I bet if I sell this house, somebody will build a house on that plot of land."' She made a mug of tea and wandered around the sun-dappled patch of land which forms part of the protected Dulwich Estate. 'I came back to the office and booked a place on a weekend course run by the National Self Build and Renovation Centre,' she says. 'That gave me the momentum I needed to start the ball rolling.'

Soon after, Corinne was diagnosed with cancer. 'It made me look at things in a totally different light,' she says. 'I'm not a risk taker – I'm quite a measured person, but when I was diagnosed, I thought, if I don't get this project off the ground now, I never will. It spurred me on and kept my mind occupied.'

Corinne's brief to her architect, Simon Skeffington, was succinct: 'Build me a home that will simplify my life.' Recently divorced, she envisaged an exquisitely designed, well-insulated home with smart technology that required virtually no maintenance. Over the next 18 months, the constraints of the wooded plot and the disparity between Corinne's budget and ambition (memorably described by her architect as 'a lager budget for champagne tastes'), meant that the design went through many iterations throughout the whole design and build process.

Plans were swiftly approved and in 2021 the construction of Corinne's highly bespoke home began apace. The three-storey triangular design included three bedrooms on the ground floor, a high-end kitchen and dining room on the first floor and a lofty living space and terrace at the top of the house. Simon's business partner, construction specialist Julian Cotet, oversaw the build, which took just eight months to complete.

Despite the frenetic pace, Corinne could not fault the build process: 'Everybody was really proud of the build from the beginning,' she says. 'The house has a really good vibe and I think that's because everybody put such a lot of effort and love into it – even the room that houses all my plumbing and electrics is beautifully finished.' Corinne attributes this to the amazing team and the regular supply of lollies, ice cream, cookies and cool drinks she provided, but it is as much to do with her decisiveness: 'I'm a really good decision maker: I'll research something, I'll talk it through, and then – once I've made my decision – I won't change my mind. I think it made Simon and Julian's job a lot easier,' she says.

When Corinne moved into her new home, she describes it as 'a pinch me moment that went on for months. I couldn't believe how everything had come together. I was just in awe of it. I still am.' In every room, carefully considered windows frame verdant views of the woodland plot. In the first floor kitchen,

an 11-m (36-ft) expanse of glass sets you among the branches. 'I can't get rid of visitors,' says Corinne – a professional chef. 'I want to go out, but everyone just wants to come round!'

From the cushions to the exterior planting, every detail had been perfected by Corinne, who worked a 72-hour week to ensure she could realise her ambition. 'The planting was top of my wish list,' she says. 'I know what it's like to put these things off year after year, and I just didn't want to wait any more.'

Corinne's exacting taste did equate to an overspend. When the fixed price contract crept up from £600,000 to £678,000, Corinne had to reconsider the sale of her home next door. 'I had intended to keep it as an income for the future, but ultimately, I had to ask myself what I wanted from this next stage of my life, and again it came back to simplifying things,' she explains. 'It was about freeing myself up and being able to enjoy my life. Once I'd made the decision to sell the house, I was quite happy to do that.'

The simplicity that Corinne craved is reflected in her enjoyment of this healing space. 'Last winter, the trees right outside were covered in snow and all I could do was sit in a chair and look at them,' she recalls. In spring and summer, she is within touching distance of the dense woodland canopy; in autumn, when the branches become bare, all of London's skyline is revealed. 'The views are magic from every room,' she says. 'I will never tire of them.'

The Long View

It is sometimes not easy to disentangle the architectural value of a building from its personal narrative. This is understandable – and often desirable – given that buildings are for people to use. In Corinne's case they were tightly bound. Her recent story of a struggle to earn, divorce, illness and continuing treatment made at times for a dark story. But her radiant positivity was an example that shone through the difficulties of building. As seems so often the case, the palpable energy in the finished structure more than equalled the human energy that had gone into its making.

And the architecture was inspired, too. The triangular site had initially suggested a compromised outcome of an end of terrace home diagonally amputated. Instead, the diagonal became the principal long wall of the building and Simon Skeffington's design borrowed views wherever it could, from a rooftop terrace over treetops towards the city, and out of huge sheets of glass into the ecology of what appeared to be urban jungle, in order to suggest the luxuries of space, privacy and connection. This is a house that points to how we can revitalise cities by building with big vision on impossibly small pieces of land.

2022
—
Scandi Villa
—
South Manchester

•	Episode aired	2022
•	Location	Greater Manchester
•	Owner(s)	Colin and Adele
•	Architect(s)	Vasco Trigueiros
•	Build cost	approx. £1.7 million (as of 2022)

There are many recommended ways of building a house. All seek to minimise failure and streamline delivery. You can buy a kit home from Poland or Germany and enjoy a hassle-free experience with no money woes. You can ask for a turnkey delivery from a respected main contractor. You can insure yourself by employing a quantity surveyor, engineer and architect who all know each other (and the planners to boot), who work in your area and know it, and all its tradespeople, well.

None of these routes appealed to Colin and Adele. They wanted an extraordinary, exuberant deco-inspired, Scandi eco-house designed and built in an unusual and creative way, as if having your Brazilian architect based in Sweden, and the timber framing company based in Latvia doesn't present enough challenges.

What followed was a memorable and as to be expected spiralling-cost and stop-start project, fed by Colin and Adele's energy and by money he would make from his career as a film and television producer. It was all skin of teeth, wide-eyed, nerve-shredding, hair-standing-on-the-neck stuff and cost far too much money. But there is no doubt that the building they have, despite all the hyphens, is a fine finished thing. Its curved glass walls ooze glamour, the layouts are magical, the private suite enticing and the furnishings point to a day in interior design that is yet to happen, perhaps sometime around 2035.

We don't often feast our cameras on expansive villas and luxurious homes. It is a rare treat. When we do indulge our curiosity in such a house as Colin and Adele's we find ourselves seduced, pampered and charmed. At the end of a day's filming we're reluctant to leave – as we head back to the hotel for a cold shower.

2023

—

House in the Woods

—

South Herefordshire

•	Episode aired	2023
•	Location	Herefordshire
•	Owner(s)	Lucinda
•	Architect(s)	Elly Deacon-Smith/Architype
•	Build cost	£178,000 (to date)

Lucinda began enjoying her Grand Design long before it was even built. 'It was just a patch of scrubland in the garden, but we decided to celebrate a birthday there with a big picnic,' she recalls. Together with friends and family, she worked out roughly where the front door and dining table would one day be situated, unfurled a rug and enjoyed her first feast 'in' the house.

That first al fresco experience was later followed by a candlelit dinner party long before the house was finished: 'It was September, so it was a bit chilly – but it was a clear night, and we could see stars through the section of the roof that hadn't been built yet. That was fun!'

Along with the al fresco dining, Lucinda has enjoyed every process of building a low impact woodland home in her garden in South Herefordshire. As her son remarked during filming: 'Most people build houses to live in, but it's almost as if you are building a house for the joy of building a house ...'

For Lucinda, a retired furniture maker, the house represents the culmination of a lifetime of making things: her 'imagination made real'. Lovingly and sustainably crafted on her own patch of woodland and to her own schedule, it also embodies Lucinda's deep seated respect for the environment. She helped set up some of the first projects that promoted responsibly sourced timber, projects that led to the founding of the Forestry Stewardship Council. 'A lot of people hand the building of their homes over to a contractor and it's all over quite quickly,' Lucinda explains. 'Mine's a different sort of build.'

The process began in the summer of 2020 and continues to this day at an unhurried pace. As Lucinda points out, without the constraints of a day job or a young family to raise, 'the luxury of time has reduced the stress of the build enormously'.

An unrestricted schedule has also enabled Lucinda to explore construction methods that reflect her commitment to sustainability. The tiny proportion of concrete to timber used has resulted in a carbon negative structure built to Passivhaus principles. The builders were constrained to a small area of the site to

prevent any unnecessary scarring of the landscape. Furthermore, heavy machinery went no further than the end of the drive in order to protect the roots of established trees. For both soil and stress levels, this has been a low impact build.

Lucinda's grown-up children, Dan and Rosie, were on site for much of the project. For Lucinda, the presence of our film crew enriched that experience: 'It was something we were all doing together, which added to our family bonding experience,' she says. As lockdown descended, Lucinda welcomed the company of the crew who enlivened the secluded site. Dan and Rosie's local friends also helped boost morale: 'Although at the time, they weren't allowed to see them socially because of the pandemic, they were allowed to work as labourers, digging holes and shifting concrete on a building site together.'

Lucinda has applied her furniture maker's precision to every aspect of the build. But she reflects: 'Although I've thoroughly enjoyed the research and the decision-making process – if I get anything wrong, then I have to live with those mistakes knowing they are mine alone.'

Even the more mundane jobs – such as nailing 10,500 cedar shingles to the exterior – have been (mostly) relished by Lucinda. 'When you're out there on the scaffold and it's freezing and there are still another 5,000 to go, it could get tough,' she admits. 'But, as long as it wasn't too cold, it became quite a meditative process.'

We completed final filming in October 2023. As of early 2024, Lucinda is still living in the family house below the new site, waiting for the builders to return before she can start work on the interior walls and furniture. The enforced pause has given her 'breathing space' – time to make more models and to think deeply about what it might be like to live inside the home she has so carefully crafted.

'I'm hoping it won't be a series of superficial wow factors but work as an integrated whole,' she says. 'I just want people to come in and think that the building has a good feeling to it. It raises my spirits whenever I walk up to it, and I hope that – eventually – it will do the same when I'm living inside.'

The Long View

The Passive House Institute guards the values and standards of passive, energy efficient construction, known as Passivhaus standards, with vigilance. Although Britain has lost its once rigorous building standards of nearly 20 years ago, which included both the target for, and a route map to, zero carbon in construction by 2016, that objective paired with that date now seems as quaint as it is worryingly overdue.

Passivhaus status is still an important construction performance metric, however. Across Europe there are now more than 40,000 Passive Houses and the influence is growing. As of January 2025 all new homes in Scotland must be built to an equivalent standard and other North European countries are following suit.

Lucinda's project is important. She's aiming for Passivhaus standards and yet she has commissioned from her architect a building that is also elegant and which she has made with great precision. She is a designer and furniture maker, and so has conjured in her woodland a synthesis of beauty, craft and performance. Passive never looked more attractive.

2023
—
Passive House Premium
—
North Cotswolds

•	Episode aired	2023
•	Location	Warwickshire
•	Owner(s)	Duncan and Liz
•	Architect(s)	Seymour-Smith Architects/Atelier73
•	Build cost	approx. £1.25 million (to date)

Much as this building is important and progressive, much as it sets a template for future housing of all kinds, there is one important aspect of it that needs dealing with first, one elephant that is not so much in the room as is the room. This house is really big. It is big enough to accommodate several large families, big enough to be a village hall with its own separate badminton court. In an age when resource use is at the fore of conversations about sustainability, this house seems, at first, wilful and profligate.

But look more closely and you realise its use of cladding, concrete and laminated timber is abstemious. The language of this building is agricultural and basic, and for its size it sips at resources. Meanwhile it is designed and constructed to properly gulp light (and therefore the solar gain of infrared radiation) in winter, while shading its occupants from the heat of summer. It may be big, but it is not wasteful.

And returning to its wider importance, this house was designed to Passivhaus Premium standards, meaning that not only must it conform to stringent Passivhaus principles (which include standards for resource use and embodied carbon, energy use and airtightness) but it must generate more energy than it uses. In this case, Duncan and Liz estimated that their home will generate enough energy for their use and for four other homes besides.

That very idea, of generating surplus, giving rather than taking, has huge implications for the future of housing in the UK. It suggests that our homes and streets could become, in effect, power stations; that with a variety of renewable technologies (principally solar) our dependency on centralised energy distribution could diminish to a point where its generation is held in reserve for much of the time; that communities could literally empower themselves; and that we could, as a nation, slash our carbon emissions. This is the first home to demonstrate that very powerful thought.

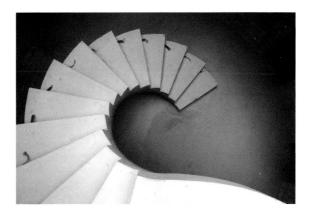

Honourable Mentions

Paying tribute to more
distinctive houses from
across the 25 years.

Threshing Barn
Surrey

Episode aired	2003
Owner(s)	Philip and Angela
Architect(s)	Damien Blower/Elspeth Beard

Revisiting an old project can be sometimes a disappointment, sometimes plain familiar and occasionally happily surprising. Going back to Philip and Angela's barn proved to be a rediscovery of the building's beauty. I had forgotten how strange and wonderful the building is: redolent of a giant wasps' nest but one built for humans. There is a poignancy in the protective and caring nature of this refuge. For as long as I've known them, Philip has been ill. It is not fanciful to say that the building has sustained them both across the 21 years it has been their home. A significant part of their objective was to make a home which was healthy and clean as much as ecological and high tech. This building radiates wellbeing and happiness and continues to look after them. Houses rarely have such a strong aura.

German Kit House
Esher

Episode aired	2004
Owner(s)	David and Greta
Architect(s)	Peter Huf

This project was fascinating for many reasons but its principal delight lay in its owners. To talk to David and Greta was a conversational deep dive into twentieth-century design, an exploration of the powerful ideas that produced the furniture, exhibition, architecture and fashion of post-war Britain. This is a world that they both freely inhabited, having lived in an architect-designed organic timber home from the early 1960s (it occupied the same site as their Huf house and was collapsing around them). But regardless of their interests and history, David and Greta were delightful. 'Were', because David sadly passed away in 2021. The house is a fitting tribute to him, replete with his paintings, sculptures and 'Huf'-inspired mosaic panels. Greta, I hope, still sees him 'tingling with excitement' all around her in these works.

Modernisation of Elizabethan Farmhouse Gloucester

Episode aired	2005
Owner(s)	Jeremy and Louise
Architect(s)	Toby Falconer

Wrangling an old building into modern use can prove a fastidious, fraught and delicate operation. In 'restoring' an old place people often kill the building, expunging all the idiosyncratic bendy bits and putting in new inappropriate details and materials in the name of 'design'. The result is often a fudged mess. What I liked about this project was the way Louise and Jeremy trod lightly, respecting the fibre and structure, the skin and the soul of the old farmhouse and took a naturally cautious approach, guided by their conservation architect. There was plenty of clear distinction between repairs, replacement and new, which always helps. Whenever I visited I felt I could read the long narrative of the place like a book, to which Jeremy and Louise had added their own gentle post-script.

Farmhouse Chalet Renovation Les Gets, France

Episode aired	2006 (revisit; first episode 2004)
Owner(s)	Nicky and James
Architect(s)	Daniel de Lavay/Henriette Salvesen

There is a design talent that escapes the British. We are not good at taking the best qualities of a simple life and glamorising them. The French understand that good food, wine, place, family and company are the ingredients of day-to-day happiness. The Italians have added music, aesthetics and a small dollop of silliness to become world leaders in exporting a polished version of *la vita povera*. We Anglo-Saxons confuse quantity with quality, resulting in buildings that are too big, stuffed with expensive meaningless things. It's the design equivalent of fast food versus Tuscan bean soup. Nicky's alpine home is not British because she isn't either. Her European roots and instinct for the noble potency of simple rustic ideas ensure that interior designer Nicky's work feels rooted in reality and the activities and values of a place.

Gentrified Fourteenth-century Peel Tower
Yorkshire

Episode aired	2007
Owner(s)	Francis and Karen
Architect(s)	Francis Shaw

Academic and English Heritage Inspector of Ancient Monuments Dr Keith Emerick was Francis and Karen's case officer for the Peel when he was also contributing towards *English Heritage's Conservation Principles*, a 2008 document which set out a radical set of approaches to heritage. The Peel became something of a test case, on the basis that, had it not been rebuilt, it would have soon disappeared into a pile of rubble. This pragmatic approach allowed Francis and Karen to weave childhood dreams in among the ancient stones, to add inventively here and there, to contemporise and to creatively reimagine spaces. A very different approach was taken at Astley Castle where managed decay, a clear narrative of building and crisp twenty-first-century additions are strikingly drawn. But the methodology of both take their place among the many imaginative ways in which we now look after our built heritage.

Contemporary Family House
Bath

Episode aired	2008
Owner(s)	Jonny and Tiffany
Architect(s)	Craig Underdown

How do we develop and build homes off site in factories rather than trying to put them up bit by bit in the rain? As ever, many Europeans and the Canadians have stolen a march on us here. When we made *The Streets*, our series about affordable self-build in the UK, we were repeatedly embarrassed by European companies who, every week, would deliver another bespoke Passive House on the back of a lorry, as if it were easy. The challenge of all prefab construction lies in the art of stitching a building into place without it looking like part of a Lego kit. Baufritz in Germany has just about perfected the art of seemingly infinite versatility: its home for Jonny and Tiffany was made in a modern factory but is rooted in character in Georgian Bath.

Twenty-first-century Farmhouse
Marlborough

Episode aired	2009
Owner(s)	Andrew and Meryl
Architect(s)	Timothy Bennett

Andrew and Meryl's house, built in open countryside outside
any planning envelope, exists thanks to a benign law that allows
farmers to put up a home for themselves or an employee if they
can demonstrate a professional need; not too difficult since the
original farmhouse where they lived was separated from the
farm by a busy road and a housing estate. Andrew had already
proved his credentials as a patron of design by building his
stockman a pointy looking oak-framed house. Probably the most
interesting agricultural worker's house in the country, it augured
well for the quality of the new farmhouse – made of the next
generation of wooden framing materials: laminated timber.
The result is in my view an extraordinary and confident
statement about farming and its future (rare in agriculture)
that is optimistic and progressive.

Modest Contemporary Home
Woodbridge

Episode aired	2010
Owner(s)	Lucie
Architect(s)	Jerry Tate

An architect acquaintance once said: 'Never make friends with
your client. Not until the house is built.' Sound advice – but what
happens when the architect is already a great friend? In the
case of Jerry Tate and Lucie, the answer is great things. Lucie
did not have a fortune to spend but wanted a sustainable home
that fitted her site next to a genteel 1960s development. Jerry's
answer was a magical twenty-first-century take on the chalet
bungalow, built of insulated timber cassettes to provide a huge
roof space into which Lucie and her children could amply fit two
storeys and the rest. And, as a friend and constant architectural
companion, Jerry was able to guide and support Lucie through
the design and building processes, which also made the job of
filming this project almost effortless.

Hole in the Wall
Kensington

Episode aired	2011
Owner(s)	Ian and Claire
Architect(s)	Ian Hogarth

The long view of this house was down a polite Kensington mews along which neighbours took a dim view of construction traffic. To the west the tight site was slung hard against a boundary with a railway. Planning dictated a maximum height so there was nowhere to go but down, and even then they hit an underground stream. Architects call these negatives 'boundary constraints' and 'exigencies'. For Ian and Claire – experienced practitioners – they were simply reflexive opportunities against which to build a microcosm of their family world: a teenage wing, guest suite, hotel apartment, disco, gym, wellness spa and sculpture garden. And in the city, where the exigencies can be so tight and the views limited, the creation of worlds within spaces is an art in itself.

Camden Workshop
Camden

Episode aired	2012
Owner(s)	Henning and Alice
Architect(s)	Henning Stummel

It is rare to meet serial house builders, especially when they're architects. Alice and Henning are on a creative experimental adventure. Their latest red tin new build house in London made the finals of House of the Year and their previous home, which we followed for television, was equally a live–work space (from which Henning runs his practice), a fascinating exploration of how to convert a run-down light industrial shed. This was a visual essay in making small timber structures, that could be insulated and cosy, within a larger open space – the problem being that older factories and warehouses don't always lend themselves to high performance retro fitting or to easy sub-division. The resulting building, like all of Henning's architecture, is seemingly easy to read and playful while also packing a punch of inventiveness and wit. Just what our cities need.

Cob House
East Devon

Episode aired	2013
Owner(s)	Kevin and Rose
Architect(s)	Barry Jobson

Kevin is the King of Cob. He believes his home is one of the largest manmade cob structures on the planet. In *The Craftsman*, the philosopher Richard Sennett writes how it takes around 10,000 hours to master a skill – whether as a woodworker, parent or software programmer – beyond which the sign of an expert is their ability to play and even joke in the language of their craft. Kevin takes play seriously to create new beauty in the language of his material. And in this home, he has experimented with hybrid arrangements of cob with modern insulation, sophisticated glazing systems and heat recovery ventilation to push at what is possible. He should be congratulated for evolving the language and the science of building in this ancient and zero carbon material.

Cliff Top House
North Wales

Episode aired	2014
Owner(s)	Rob and Kay
Architect(s)	John Boardman

For a white Modernist villa to make a *Grand Designs* episode, it has to be really exemplary. It has to reflect the best this canon of architecture has to offer and it has to evolve the contribution that Modernism has made. Rob and Kay's home, designed by John Boardman in Manchester, was nominated for House of the Year and pushes at the boundaries of what a white box can do. It is energy efficient, it is designed to deal with Atlantic weather and the erosion of the adjacent coastline, it is modest in scale but it punches well above its weight, while it also curbs its own enthusiasms behind a tall stone wall adjacent to a footpath that runs through the Site of Special Scientific Interest in which it sits. It is clever Modernism.

Cow Shed
South Somerset

Episode aired	2015
Owner(s)	Vicky and Ed
Consult. Arch.	Wiebke Rietz of Alchemilla Architects

Looking back at the first episode of this project, you might be forgiven for thinking that Ed and Vicky's adventures in sustainability (which this project amounted to) were open ended and not fully formed. Revisiting them in the early 2020s brought their project into clearer focus. The house (a brick and concrete former milking parlour overlooking the valleys of south Somerset) was always a retrofit of timber, insulation, straw bale construction and cob. However, these approaches have matured and their site is now a full synthesis of ecological building techniques, organic farming, sustainable cookery school, biodiverse landscape management and an additional home for Vicky's father. Their house is not so much a building as an evolving story.

Woodland House
Essex

Episode aired	2016
Owner(s)	David and Michelle
Architect(s)	David Parsons

The collaboration of architects with artists is always energetic and some architects seek out these relationships. Perhaps all the better that artist Michelle and architect David are also partners in life. Their joint project is both home and studio. In fact, the journey to, through and beyond the house can be read with the studio as the destination and the sequence of experiences on the way there as a set of controlled experiments with light. It is a thoughtful, modest and magical building which engaged them so much they are now repeating the experience with a second version of this house. We need to be repeatedly reminded by projects like this that great architecture can be affordable and small. It just needs to be thoughtful, considered and creative.

Box House
East London

Episode aired	2017
Owner(s)	Joe and Lina
Design	Joe

When an engineer builds a house, two things are almost guaranteed. The first is that the thing will be carefully built. The second is that it will inevitably offer its maker an irresistible chance to innovate. No engineer I know, when presented with a pile of materials and an opportunity to make something original, can resist the opportunity for invention. Joe is no exception, and his house bristles with spacesaving ideas and cutting edge technology. It is a small container for big ideas. He and Lina should also be congratulated for putting their money and faith into a part of London which needed a little lifting. Regeneration of places never starts with government agencies; it starts when the artists – and the engineers – move in.

Twins Houses
Sheffield

Episode aired	2018
Owner(s)	Nik and Emma, Jon and Ali
Arch. Designer	Abel Hinchliffe - CODA Studios

All good buildings are their own prototypes because each one responds to its time and place and its residents. So it was fascinating to watch twins Nik and Jon produce two adjacent variants on their prototype. Their tastes are extremely close (there is no desire for much fancy or whim) but their family circumstances were different, so the differences between the homes reflect need more than desire. Theirs was a complex story to tell in an hour, with two buildings, two households and a site replete with industrial archaeology that involved the restoration of a wheel pit and a mill pond. But the brothers' closeness, their collaboration in business as well as on site, and the strong family connections to the place and to the city of Sheffield gave the film resonance and grit. And the houses are fabulous.

Round House
Lincolnshire

Episode aired	2019
Owner(s)	Paul and Amy
Architect(s)	Robert Lowe

There is a quirk in planning law that allows you to build in open countryside, but it comes with its own set of strings. Most difficult of all, many local authorities have no idea how to assess these planning applications. Fortunately, Paul and Amy navigated this difficult path, and what is so striking about their project is its reach for beauty. This comes from the elegant curves of the buildings, and the ponds, hedges and bat boxes, but principally from the extensive landscape and lake that Paul has remediated from ecologically poor farmland into a haven for wildlife. And it's clear that in his loving stewardship of the site's biodiversity, he has also found renewal by immersion, surrounding himself with life.

Cemetery Lodge
South West London

Episode aired	2021
Owner(s)	Justin
Architect(s)	Simon Gill

Some people build simply to get shelter, others to show off. Some build to provide for their loved ones, some to memorialise themselves. But few people build with a sense of legacy. Justin is one such person, whose connection to his own ancestry and sense of the future is intimately woven together. It's perhaps not a surprise that someone who can trace their family roots back five hundred years and whose family have lived on the same site in Scotland for centuries, feels more engaged with a sense of continuity and heritage. This struck home when during the course of filming Justin's project, the cameras filmed him visiting the family crypt where he found himself at home with his ancestors. As a result, his architectural journey was surprisingly confident.

Barn Conversion
Sevenoaks

Episode aired	2021
Owner(s)	Greg and Georgie
Architect(s)	Mike Kaner from Kaner Olette

Buildings can store within them enormous reserves of human energy and no little emotion. This was a film and a building that came to embody love, hope, faith, joy, resilience and renewal. The scheme was all the more powerful because it took place in lockdown and construction lay in the hands of just a few people. Greg's talent and smiling resolve and Georgie's faith and positivity had overcome so much in their lives, and of course they overcame this project as well, despite ongoing health difficulties. The lesson for us all is that building a house may be tough but there are greater and more profound challenges in the world. If you are lucky, as Greg and Georgie were, all that embodied human energy in the building will repay you over time, with interest.

Modular House
Tunbridge Wells

Episode aired	2022
Owner(s)	Kate and Rob
Design	Boutique Modern

We should really be building more homes in a modular way, off site in factories. By doing this, we could deliver more affordable housing and produce buildings efficiently and in the dry. Firms leading the way include Top Hat, Urban Splash and Boutique Modern, who built Kate and Rob's house in Kent. This is a timber, super-insulated, airtight home that comes with its own QR code, an online instruction manual and full traceability for every component. It is how twenty-first-century sustainable building should be: prefabricated and not expensive, with standardised components and volumes, but sensitively custom tailored to its site and to its owners. More like this, please.

Tree House
Scunthorpe

Episode aired	2023
Owner(s)	Danny
Architect(s)	Kate Kelly

Nothing decent would ever get built if we all succumbed to the culture of 'that'll do'. By the same token, humans can be victims of their own arrogance and vanity in the pursuit of perfection. The right route, in building, is to aim for the high peak of ambition, tread lightly as you go, don't burden yourself with luggage and be nimble. Oh, and only stop to turn round and see how high you've come; keep going. Danny embodies this philosophy. He is a hugely driven man, a super-achiever who wanted a proper piece of architecture by a pond, down a track that would also be modest, to feel like a treehouse for his children to play in, a place in which to commune with wildlife and the elements. It didn't need to be big or even be properly accessible by car. The resulting home fits that modest bill and shows us we don't need expensive sofas and ridiculous glazing to make really good buildings.

Afterword

Behind every dramatic winter scene with water droplets forming on sodden wooden beams, there is a woman or man with a camera, equally sodden, with droplets forming on the end of their nose.

We are the nose droplet people. The unsung weekly heroes on Channel 4 at 9 pm; the people whose names appear at the end of the programme – whizzing down the screen over beautiful sweeping shots of finished buildings.

I am one of the longest serving of the nose droplet people – I've worked on the show on and off in different roles for the best part of 25 years. So ... what can I tell you?

Just because you are filming, you are not special. Contractors will not make an effort to be there when they say they will just because you are filming the nation's favourite architecture series. The concrete is arriving at 8 am. We'll be there to set up at 7 am. By the time we reach lunchtime ... there's still no sign.

You get the reverse problem too. The builder on the Isle of Skye was an incredible man. Proud of his work and rightly so. This did mean that he preferred us to film each stage of the build finished, rather than the process of getting there. It meant that we often would have to turn up very, very early – learning that was the only way we'd be able to see the transformation.

Then there are filming days with big machinery ... Gene Wilder says in *Willy Wonka & the Chocolate Factory* (1971): 'If the good Lord had intended us to walk, he wouldn't have invented roller skates.' The same applies to filming big machinery processes, proximity to said processes and long lenses. I have witnessed crane tethers snap and tonnes of timber crash to the ground and been grateful to the gods of ZEISS that their supernatural glass technology allows what is small in the distance to become larger. Building sites are some of the most dangerous places you can be and anything that gets you closer to the action without needing to be close to the action is to be grateful for.

The most common question I get asked: is Kevin really as nice as he is on screen? It's an odd question. It seems to carry with it the erroneous idea that the moment the cameras cut, Mr Hyde tears off the Kevin-shaped prosthetic mask and a junior member of the production team is tied to a stake and made a blood sacrifice for failure to produce dinner at the required time. Kevin is an exceptionally thoughtful, kind and magnanimous person who is more involved in the production process than anyone I've ever worked with. He's really funny and really clever. He speaks French and Italian fluently, he is an amazing artist and has a rare ability to make the most complex technical thing sound accessible and fascinating. He is a great friend and collaborator and the reason I developed my passion for architecture.

Now, finally, the people who build, who we follow, without whom there would be no series. Building your own house is a crucible – out of which new people often emerge (along with a new home). These new people are often more empowered, confident and stronger – that's if they can survive the process, which is gruelling in the extreme.

So to all self-builders of the United Kingdom and beyond – the nose droplet people thank and salute you.

Ned Williams

Episode List

Spring 1999
Newhaven
Oxford
Brighton
Amersham
Suffolk
Cornwall
Islington
Doncaster

Autumn 2001
Farnham
Sussex
Huddersfield
Wales
Lambourn
Birmingham
London
Devon

Spring 2003
Peterborough
Chesterfield
Sussex
Surrey

Autumn 2003
Hackney
Cumbria
Hereford

Spring 2004
Waterloo
Esher
Edinburgh
Clapham
Hastings
Glasgow
Dorset

Autumn 2004
Malaga, Spain
Lot, France
Puglia, Italy
Creuse, France
Westport, Ireland
Tuscany, Italy
Les Gets, France
Alicante, Spain

Spring 2005
Peckham
Gloucester
Kent

Autumn 2005
Devon
Belfast
Exmouth
Carmarthen

Spring 2006
Killearn
Ross-on-Wye
Stirling
Ashford
Exeter

Spring 2007
Yorkshire
Hampshire
Medway
Bournemouth
Birmingham
Guildford
Cambridgeshire
London

Spring 2008
Cheltenham
Bristol
Monmouth
Midlothian
Bath
Maidstone

Spring 2009
Somerset
Chilterns
Newport
Weald of Kent
Brittany
Marlborough
Headcorn
Brighton

Autumn 2010
Isle of Wight
Cotswolds
Woodbridge
Stowmarket
Ipswich
Lizard Peninsula
West Cumbria
Lake District

Autumn 2011
Newcastle
Bromley
Tenby
Braintree
Herefordshire
Cornwall
Kensington

Autumn 2012
Southern Ireland
Hertfordshire
Brixton
River Thames
Kennington
West London
Skye
Camden

Autumn 2013
South Yorkshire
North London
York
Tiverton
Strathaven
Monmouthshire
South London
East Devon
Newbury

Autumn 2014
North Wales
North Cornwall
Milton Keynes
County Derry
South East London
Norwich
Buckinghamshire

Autumn 2015
West Sussex
East Sussex
Solent
Wyre Forest
County Antrim
South Somerset
South Downs

Autumn 2016
Gloucestershire
Horsham
South Cornwall
Essex
Bolton
Pembrokeshire
Honiton
Wirral

Autumn 2017
Malvern
Haringey
County Down
South Hertfordshire
Herne Hill
Blackdown Hills
Peak District
East London
Herefordshire II

Autumn 2018
Aylesbury Vale
Padstow
Richmond
Leominster
Sheffield
Lewes

Autumn 2019
Galloway
Lincolnshire
Warwickshire
Hull
West Suffolk
North Devon

January 2021
South West London
Sevenoaks
South Lincolnshire
Bletchley
Liskeard

Autumn 2021
Huxham
Billingshurst
Kinross
Ely
Chichester
South Lakeland
East Essex

Autumn 2022
South Manchester
Tunbridge Wells
Canterbury
Chess Valley
Derbyshire
Dunstable
Sydenham Hill

Autumn 2023
Wye Valley
Scunthorpe
Hackney Downs
South Herefordshire
North Cotswolds

Plus numerous revisits over the years.

To watch episodes, go to www.granddesigns.tv
or www.channel4.com/programmes/grand-designs

Acknowledgements

The number of people involved in the creation, nurturing and longer-term stewardship of *Grand Designs* extends into the several hundreds and I am indebted to anyone who has spent time alongside us on the journey of the last quarter century. We've compiled a list of individuals overleaf who have made a special contribution to the vitality of the series, but I also want to record in print my personal thanks to those who have inspired and entertained me on the way through.

First and foremost, Daisy Goodwin whose idea it was (and who generously wrote this book's foreword) alongside Peter Fincham who jointly pitched the series to Channel 4. From the channel itself, our first brave commissioning editor Liz Warner. Many of our commissioning editors and directors of television are mentioned by name in the list and I am particularly grateful for their enduring patience, stamina and energy. Twenty-five years on, the enthusiasm and support of Ian Katz, Emma Hardy, Alex Mahon and Ian Dunkley is undimmed.

Thanks that extend into the last millennium go to Kate Moon, Sahra Gott, Caroline at Oggadoon and Chris Hoare for their wisdom and guidance and to our first series producer John Silver and Tony Etwell on camera. Together we were able to craft the narrative and visual language of the films.

The recognisable imprimatur of *Grand Designs* was hugely enriched by the music of David Lowe and so many other great composers. It was also tailored and developed by the great phalanx of other creatives that have worked on the series: our directors and assistant producers, editors, camera ops and sound recordists (Andrew Marchant is still with us). Our series producers and executive producers deserve to be mentioned in dispatches: Fiona Caldwell, Helen Simpson, my good friend Rob Gill, Mike Ratcliffe, Madeleine Hall, Charlie Bunce, Charles Furneaux, the very lovely John Comerford and, longest of all, John Lonsdale with whom I continue to enjoy collaborating and creating. His words open this book.

Thanks to all the thousands of long-suffering builders who downed tools so that we could find a little silence to record interviews. No thanks to the manufacturers of helicopters, light aircraft and impact screwdrivers.

Huge thanks to the gifted architects of the buildings we film and to our Grand Designers themselves, the hundreds of self-builders who have so generously given their time and bared their souls in having their stories told – in return for no glory or recompense other than having an expensive-looking home video of their project. Without them there could be no series.

And with no series there would have been no *Grand Designs* babies to celebrate, no exhibition nor a magazine. There would have been no books, no *House of the Year* or *The Streets* (thanks here to my brilliant colleagues Michelle Ogundehin, Damien Burrows and Natasha Huq). No Australian, Swedish or New Zealand home-grown series either, so my heartfelt thanks go to Fremantle and its many offspring: Talkback, Naked and Boundless. Also to Richard Morey, Lee Newton, Rob Nathan, my gifted editor at *Grand Designs Magazine* Karen Stylianides (plus her predecessors) and everyone at Media 10 for breathing life into our events. Thanks too to the filmmakers and in particular the presenters of the international versions of *GD* whom I call my friends; the architects Peter Maddison, Chris Moller, Tom Webster, Professor Anthony Burke, Yasmine Ghoniem and Mark Isitt. I've learned much from them.

For this book and for gallantry, especial thanks to Nikki Frost and Fran Brotherton-Cottrell in our office for their tireless research work and fact-checking, Nell Card for her vital interviews and lively words, Jayne Stephens and Tamara Howe at Fremantle and in my office Gina, who has loyally had to deal with my vagueness and vicissitudes for over two decades. I'm especially grateful to Denise Bates at Quarto and to her team. I have worked with Denise much longer than I have been making television and have enjoyed every minute of our collaboration.

Grand Designs has become my life and come to define who I am. I've met countless people through it and enjoyed moments of bliss, pleasure and robust confrontation. Also some very cold mornings. None of this would have worked out without my agents Tracey MacLeod, Theia Nankivell, Megan Hart and everyone else at KBJ to whom I am so grateful for putting up with me and for dispensing wise counsel. And alongside them, Jane Turnbull my long-standing and long-suffering hard-bargaining literary agent.

It would also be wrong not to acknowledge the unstinting support and love of my family over the last 25 years; my children have grown to be hugely tolerant of my work and the travel involved and we are all still speaking. Each in their way has followed into architecture, journalism, design and film-making; I have failed to put them off.

And finally, the following are deserving of Long-Service Medals: my great friend Ned Williams who began work on *GD* in series one (and who is still by my side) and in our production office Helen Donovan and Amy Martin, who run the show with military precision. Without them, no series, just chaos.

To you all and the many others I have not mentioned by name, Thank You.

Kevin McCloud

Special Thanks

A very special thank you to the following, who have made *Grand Designs* such a success over the last 25 years:

Hope Abbott
Frankie Albright
Sam Al-Kadi
Tom Allright
Mike Arnott
Rob Ashpitel
Martyn Balham
Max Baring
Jonathan Barker
Sasha Bates
Alex Baxter
Lee Beard
Marc Beers
Heidi Bell
Julian Bellamy
Victoria Bennetts
Joanna Beresford
Claire Birch
Simon Bisset
Mark Bos
Emma Bowen
Danny Boyd
Lucy Brown
Charlie Bunce
Ash Burnham
Fiona Caldwell
Tammy Calow
Rebecca Chambers
Jocelyn Chandler
Michael Christmas
Simon Chu
Niki Clark
John Comerford
Adam Cooper
Fran Brotherton-Cottrell

Julian Crane
Emma Crocker
Paul Curran
Malgosia Czarniecka Lonsdale
Rob Daly
Tom Dalzell
Amelia Dare
Bethan Daunter
Anna Davies
Cicelia Deane
Sally Debonnaire
Nick Denning
Mandeep Dillon
Daniel Dimbleby
Orla Doherty
Helen Donovan
Vicky Double
Niall Downing
Drago Dragostinov
Christine Drew
Ian Dunkley
Debbie Elliott
Tony Etwell
Scarlett Ewens
Paul Fallon
Ruairi Fallon
Peter Fincham
Clare Fisher
Ita Fitzgerald
Charlotte Fitzpatrick
Daisy Fordham
Orlando Fowler
Nikki Frost
Ben Frow
Johanna Fry
Katy Fryer
Charles Furneaux
Tim Gardam
Shannon Gayle-Bartlett
Sara Geater
Rob Gill

David Goodale
Daisy Goodwin
Anna Gordon
Natasha Gordon
Nicole Gordon
Belinda Gregg
Madeleine Hall
Susanne Hamilton
Emma Hardy
Matt Hatchard
Lorraine Heggessey
Steve Hewlett
George Hill
Claire Hobday
Anita Hodgson
Charlie Hollins
Tamara Howe
Imogen Howell
Stephen Hughes
Liam Humphreys
Jay Hunt
Merryn Hunter
Nicky Hurst
Kim Husher
Walter Iuzzolino
Michael Jackson
Bob Jackson
Emma James
Ben Jamieson
Manuela Jaramillo
Julia Jarvis
Lauren Jeffery
Esther Johnson
Amy Joyce
Emma Judge
Ian Katz
Rob Kelly
Tom Kent
Alexis Kepetzis
Alicia Kerr
Elliot Kew

Harry Kind
Paul King
Hannah Kingshott
Itamar Klasmer
Karen Knowles
Ann Lalic
Keith Langley
Claire Lasko
Alex Levitschi
James Lewis
Guy Linton
Jacques Lockwood
John Lonsdale
David Lowe
Kevin Lygo
Neil Maclennan
Sam Manley
Andrew Marchant
Amy Martin
Gary McAllister
Caroline McCool
Thomas McDonald
Alex Menzies
Katia Michael
Elena Miles
Ben Mitchell
Caroline Moffat
Martin Morrison
Gareth Morrow
Sue Murphy
Hoshida Nekoo
Sammy Newman
Alex Niakaris
Beatrice Ni Bhroin
Judi O'Brien
Megan O'Leary
Damian O'Mahony
Jess Orr
Katlin Palm
Anna Palmer
Richard Parkin

Nisha Patel
Louise Penez
Gemma Praditngam
Frazer Randalls
Mike Ratcliffe
Anna Ratsey
Alannah Richardson
Anne Robinson
Debbie Robinson
Rosie Rockel
Donna Rolls
Karen Rona
Nicola Ronaghan
Livia Russell
Juanita San Miguel
Joe Saunders
Catey Sexton
Graham Sherrington
Nigel Shilton
John Silver
Helen Simpson
Clea Singh
Jennifer Stanford
Alex Steinitz
Ed Stobart
Nicki Stoker
Graham Strong
Edward Sunderland
Chris Sutherland
Claire Sweeney
Kate Teckman
Araam Tehrani
Mark Thompson
Katy Tooth
Allan Tott
Christian Trumble
Selina Tso
Cal Turner
Laura Tutt
Gareth Walker
Andrew Walmsley

Dave Walter
Joanne Walton
Liz Warner
Reece Watkinson
Victoria Westmacott
Nan Whittingham
Ned Williams
Gill Wilson
Vicky Winter
Katie Wixon-Nelson

... and to all the many hundreds of others, especially our courageous self-builders, who have contributed to the series since 1999. Many thanks.

Index

Picture Credits

Key: t = top; b = bottom.

Images copyright © the following:

Front cover, top and bottom: **Malgosia Czarniecka Lonsdale**
Back cover, top: **Aidan Monaghan/Media 10**
Back cover, bottom: **Andrew Wall/Media 10**

Interior pages:
Mark Bolton: 4, 208–209, 211; **Paula Beetlestone:** 8 –9,
180–185, 260t; **Jefferson Smith/Media 10:** 12 –17, 18–23, 56–59,
61, 62, 63, 70–75, 80–83, 94–97, 139, 143, 144–145, 255t, 255b;
Edina van der Wyck/Media 10: 24 –27, 64, 254b; **Mel Yates/
Media 10:** 28 –33, 52; **Leon Foggitt:** 34 –39; **Ben Law:** 40 –45;
Simon Foster Photography Limited: 46 –49; **Marc Evans:** 51,
55; **Alun Callender/Media 10:** 66 –69; **Elizabeth Zeschin/
Media 10:** 76 –79, 253t; **Chris Tubbs/Media 10:** 84 –87, 114–117,
166–169, 257t; **Sean Begley:** 88 –93; **Richard Hawkes:** 98 –103;
Thomas Stewart/Media 10: 104 –107; **Julian Winslow:** 109,
111, 112; **Rachael Smith/Media 10:** 113, 118–123; **Andrew Wall/
Media 10:** 124 –127, 258b; **Rachel Whiting/Media 10:** 129, 133;
Josh Kearns: 131, 132, 140, 142, 257b; **Douglas Gibb/Media 10:**
134 –137; **David Barbour/Media 10:** 146 –149, 228–231; **Aidan
Monaghan/Media 10:** 150 –155; **Paul Ryan-Goff/Media 10:**
156 –159; **Richard Chivers:** 160 –165; **Alicia Victoria | Red Maple
Photography:** 170 –175; **Matt Chisnall/Media 10:** 176 –179, 259t;
Malgosia Czarniecka Lonsdale: 186 –189, 190–197, 210, 212–217,
218–221, 222–227, 232–237, 238–241, 248–251, 259b, 262t, 262b,
263t; **Mark Bolton/Media 10:** 198 –201, 258t; **Andy Haslam/
Media 10:** 202 –207, 263b; **Graham Lucas Commons:** 242 –247;
Adrian Briscoe/Media 10: 253b; **Andrew Montgomery/Media
10:** 254t; **Dave Young/Media 10:** 256t; **Jade Curtis/Media 10:**
256b; **Fiona Walker-Arnott/Media 10:** 260b, 261